MANDALAS FOR KIDS

A COLORING JOURNEY INTO IMAGINATION AND INSPIRATION

This Book belongs to:

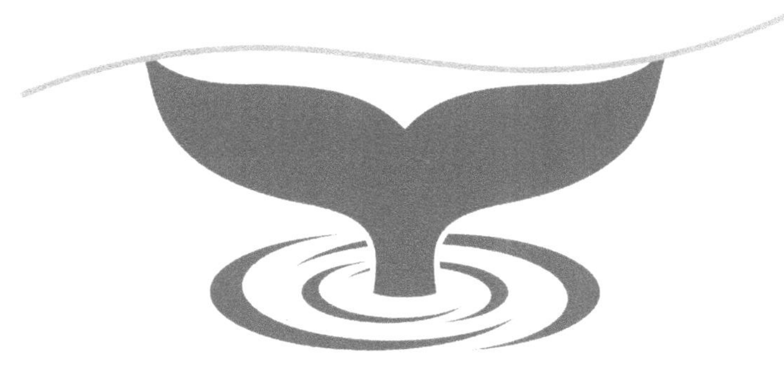

BIBI LEBLANC

BEATE KUMAR

Book 6 in the **Culture to Color**® Mandala Series

Printed in the USA

First Edition

Cover Design & Interior by
Culture to Color, LLC®

ISBN: 978-1-959924-06-7

To order in bulk contact publisher,
CultureToColor.com

For more information, visit:
CultureToColor.com

CS@CultureToColor.com
386-309-2632

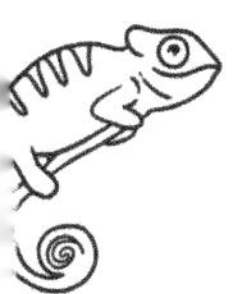
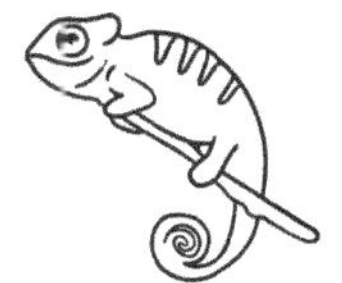

Welcome to
Mandalas for Kids

Hi there,

Get ready to embark on an enchanting journey
of colors and creativity.

Inside these magical pages, you'll find 52 unique designs
featuring playful animals, mesmerizing unicorns,
and inspiring quotes.

Let your imagination soar as you add your colors
to each mandala, and watch them come to life!

So grab your favorite coloring pencils,
and let the coloring adventure begin!

We hope you have as much fun coloring this book
as we did creating it for you!

With ♡ from our homes to yours,

Bibi & Beate

P.S. We would love to see your colored images.
Please send them to us at bibi@culturetocolor.com
or post them on social media with hashtag
#culturetocolor

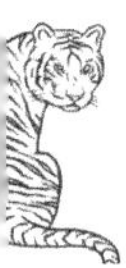

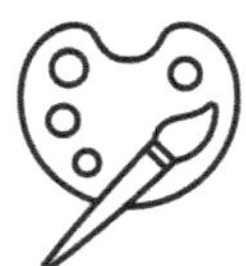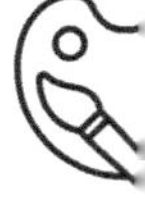

BENEFITS OF COLORING PAGE

If you include coloring in your daily routine, you will find it has many benefits for you, the coloring artist. To name just a few, coloring can:

IMPROVE FOCUS

Coloring requires repetition and attention to detail. It opens up your brain's frontal lobe, which controls organizing and problem-solving, and allows you to focus on the activity rather than your worries.

REDUCE STRESS AND ANXIETY

Coloring relaxes the fear center (amygdala) in your brain, putting you in a state similar to meditation. Coloring helps remove irritating thoughts and allows the creative mind to run free and relax.

IMPROVE SLEEP

Coloring as your bedtime ritual instead of using electronics can lead to a better night's sleep. The light emitted by electronic devices lowers the level of melatonin, your sleep hormone, whereas coloring does not affect your melatonin level.

You can take coloring supplies anywhere. And you don't have to be an artist or an expert to color and create something beautiful. Seeing your finished coloring page provides a sense of accomplishment.

Tag us with your colored pages and #CultureToColor

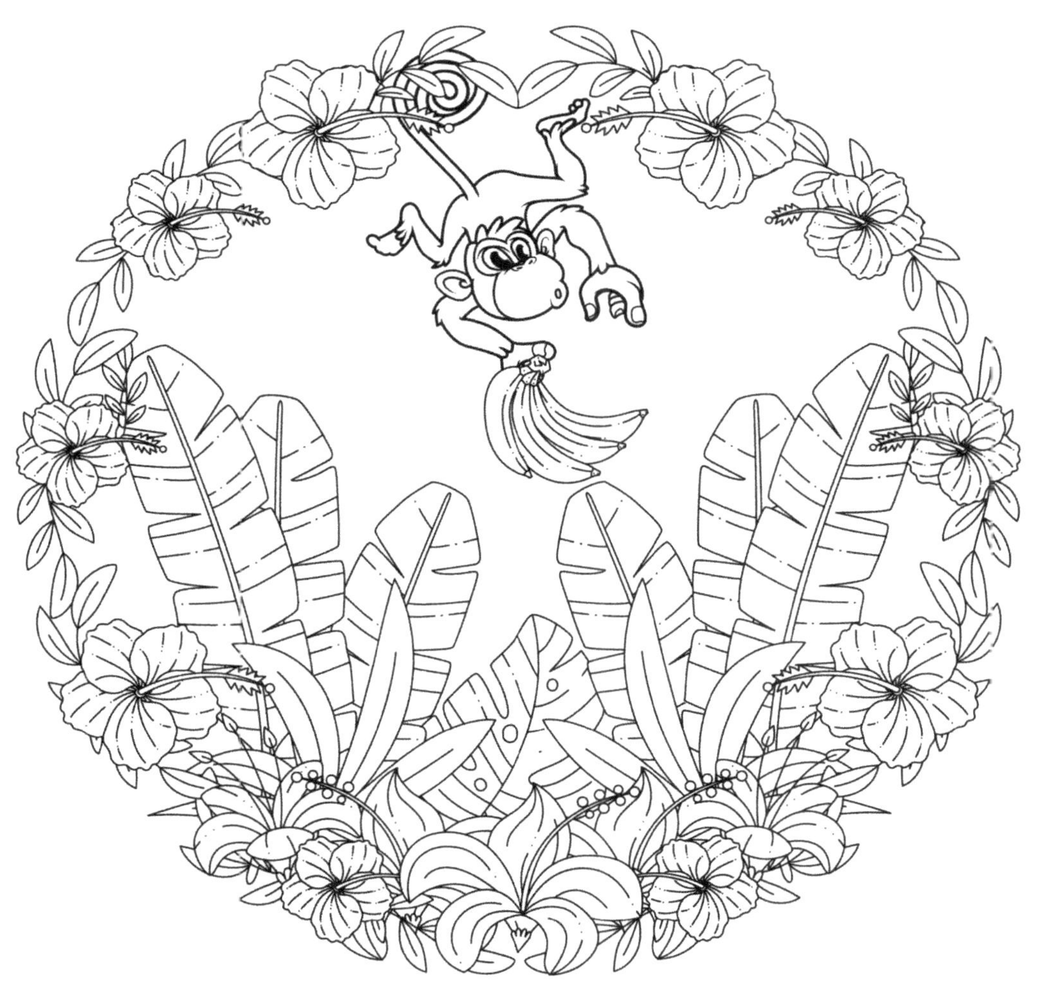

"A TRUE FRIEND IS THE GREATEST OF ALL BLESSINGS."
FRANCOIS DE LA ROCHEFOUCAULD

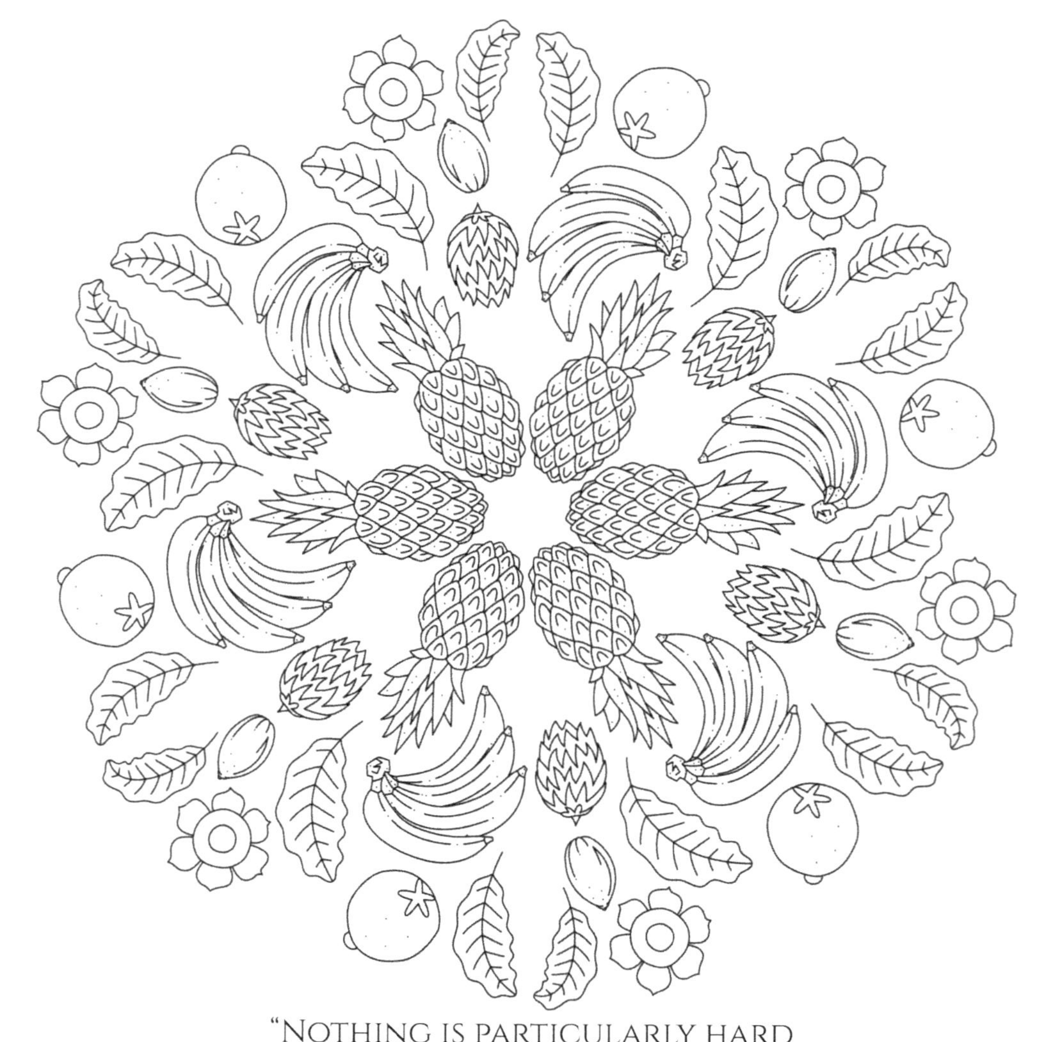

"NOTHING IS PARTICULARLY HARD
IF YOU BREAK IT INTO SMALL JOBS."
HENRY FORD

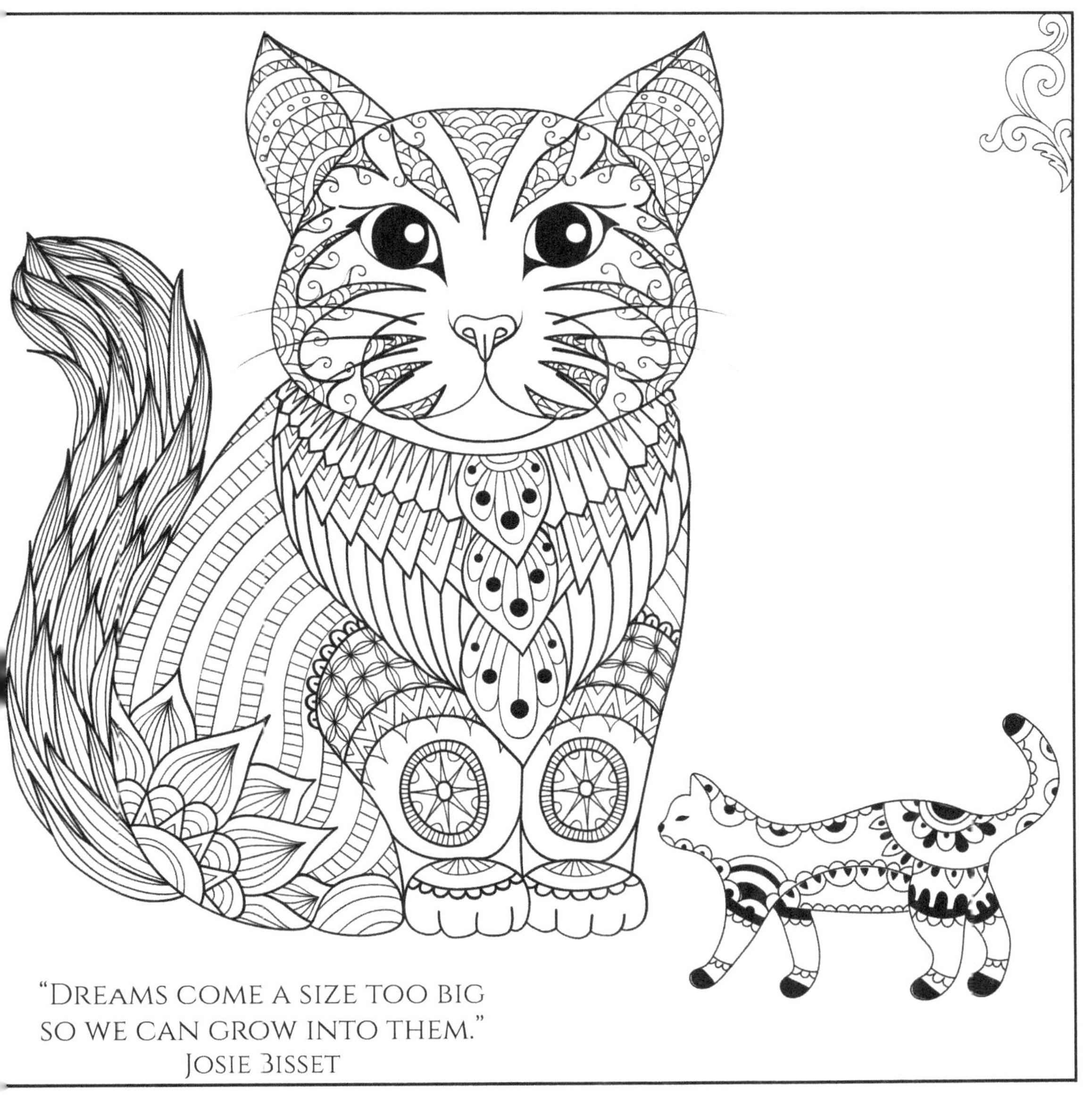

"DREAMS COME A SIZE TOO BIG
SO WE CAN GROW INTO THEM."
JOSIE BISSET

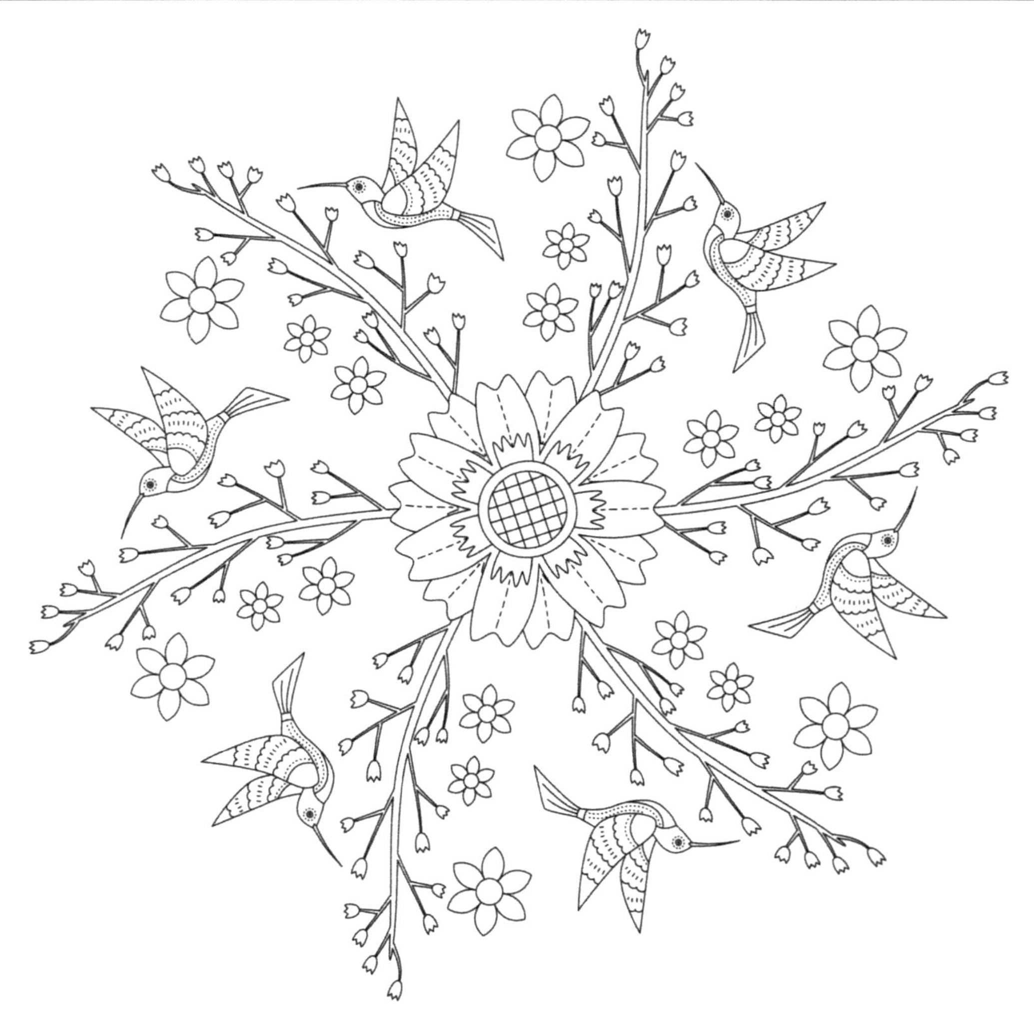

"THE EXPERT IN ANYTHING WAS ONCE A BEGINNER."
HELEN HAYES

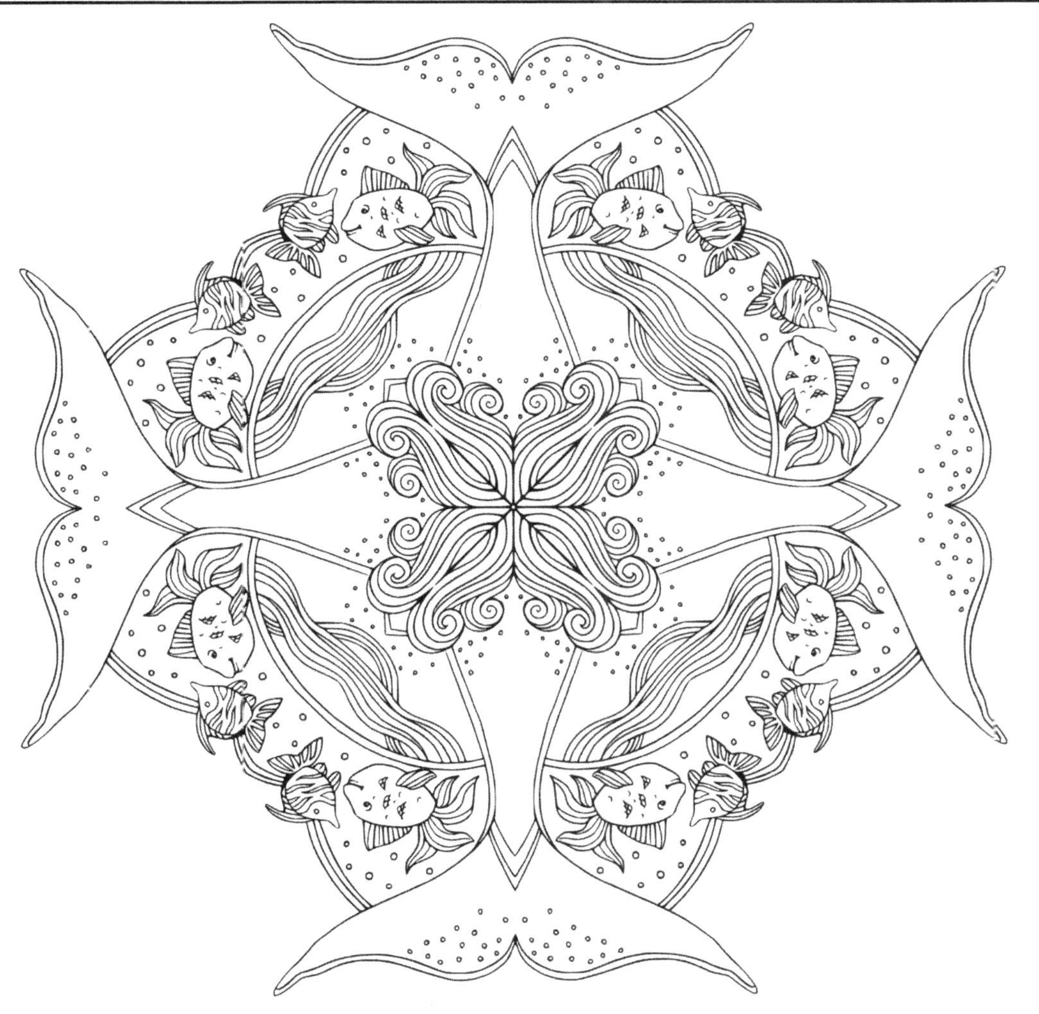

"Never say never, because limits, like fear,
are just an illusion."
Michael Jordan

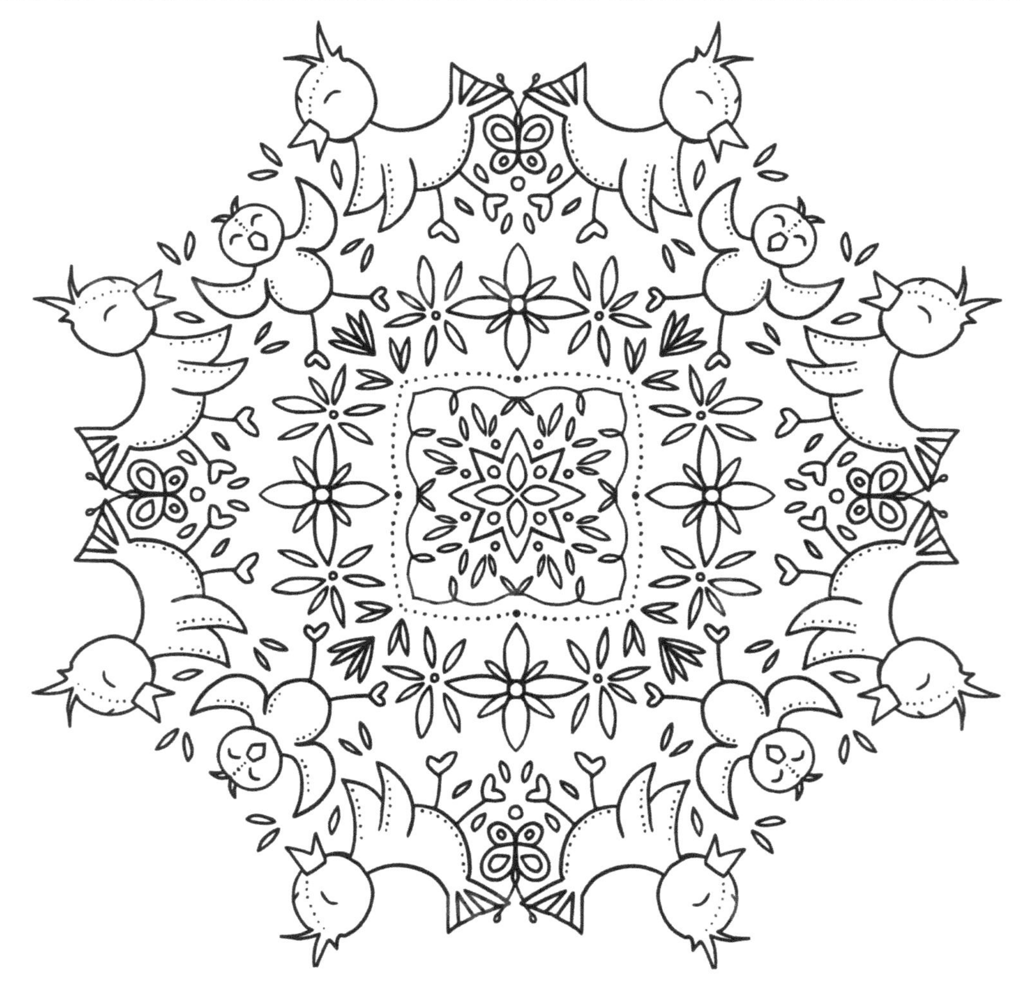

"THE KIDS WHO ASK **WHY**
ARE THE ONES WHO ARE GOING TO CHANGE THE WORLD."
NEAL THOMPSON

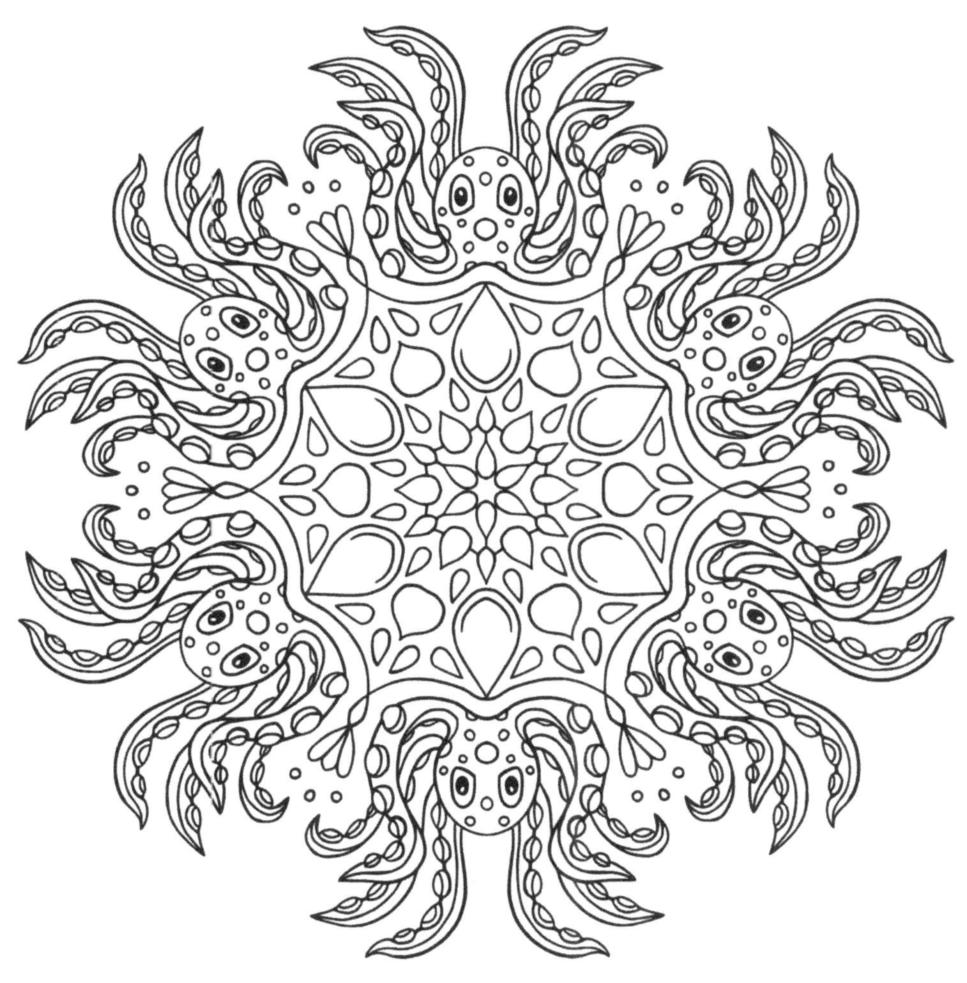

"The future belongs to those
who believe in the beauty of their dreams."
Eleanor Roosevelt

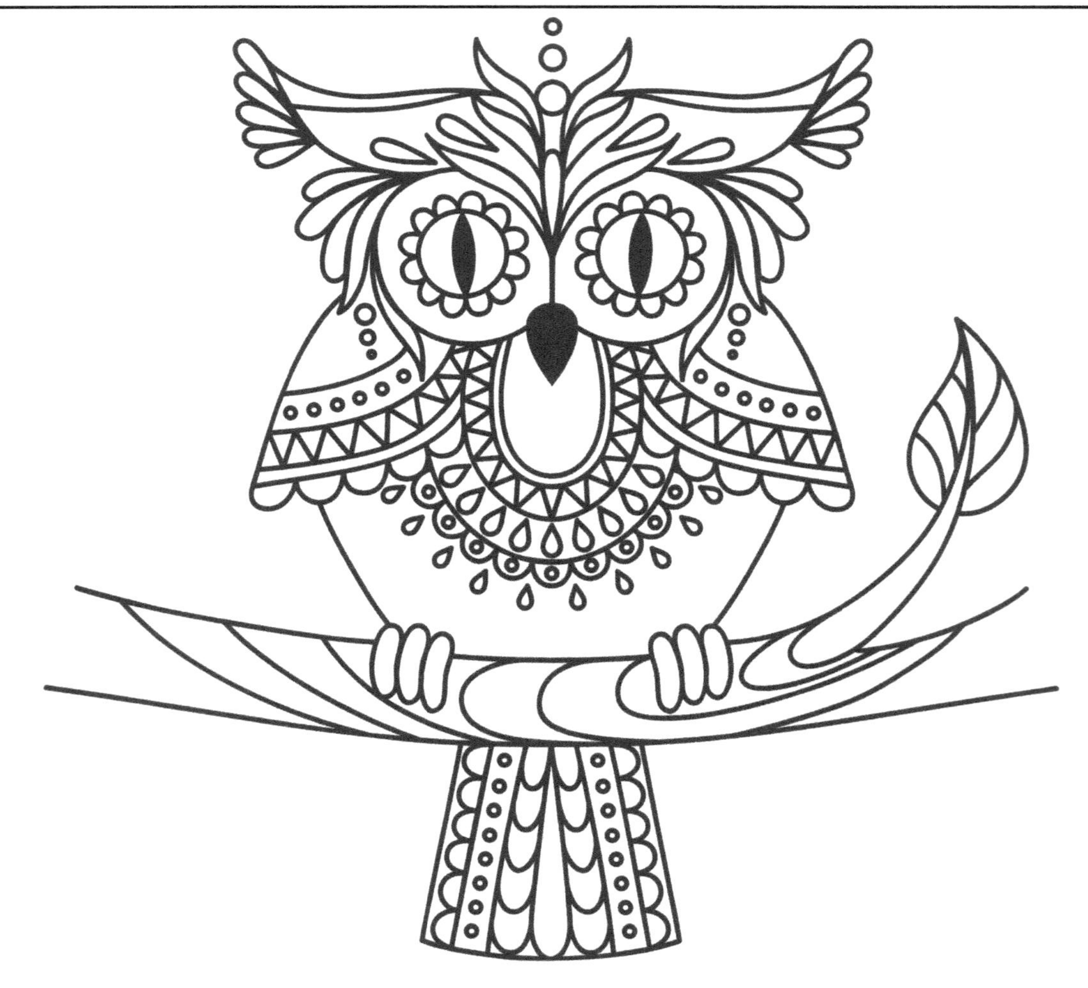

"WHY DO WE FALL?
SO WE CAN LEARN TO PICK OURSELVES BACK UP."
BATMAN

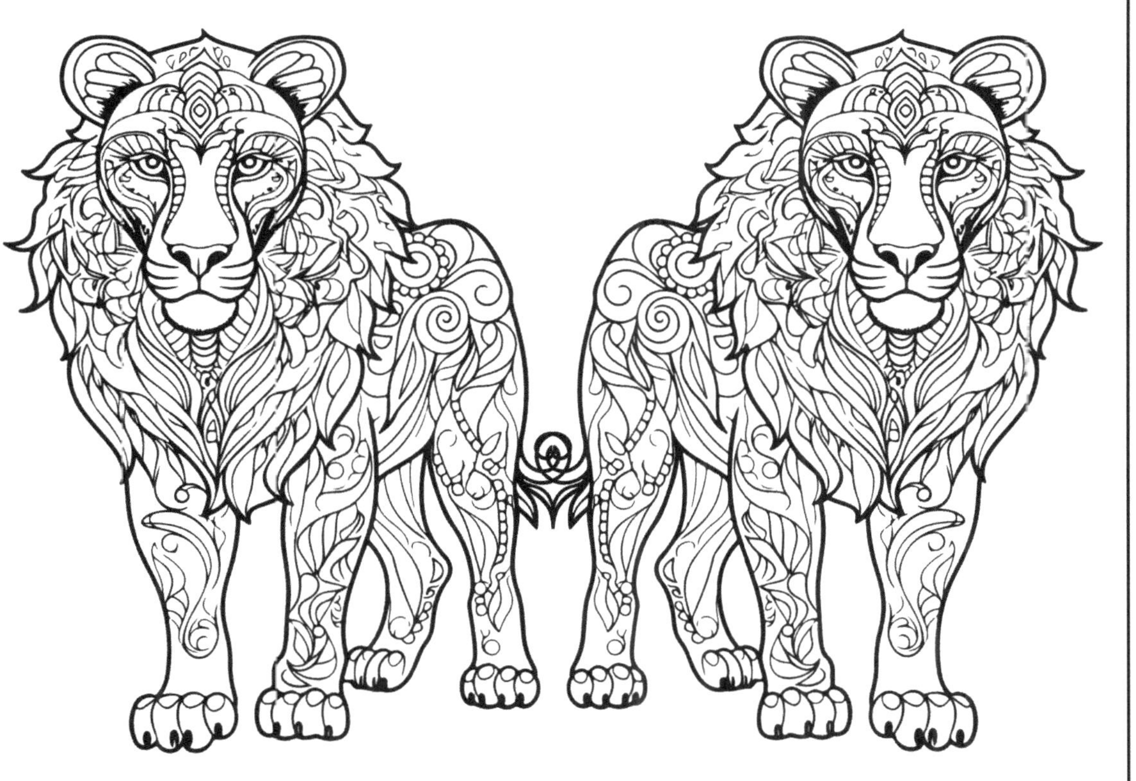

"Look up at the stars and not down at your feet.
Try to make sense of what you see and wonder about
what makes the universe exist.
Be curious."
Stephen Hawking

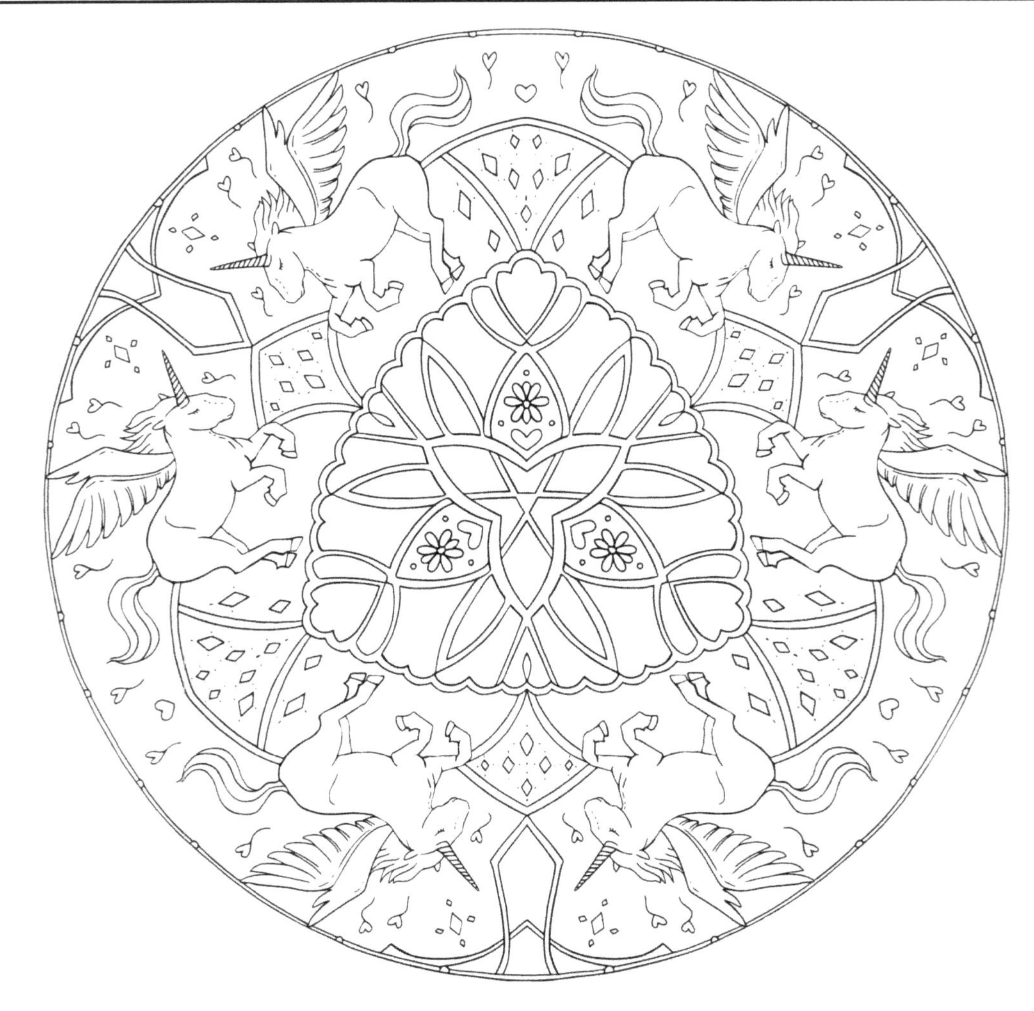

"YOU MUST DO THE THINGS YOU THINK YOU CANNOT DO."
ELEANOR ROOSEVELT

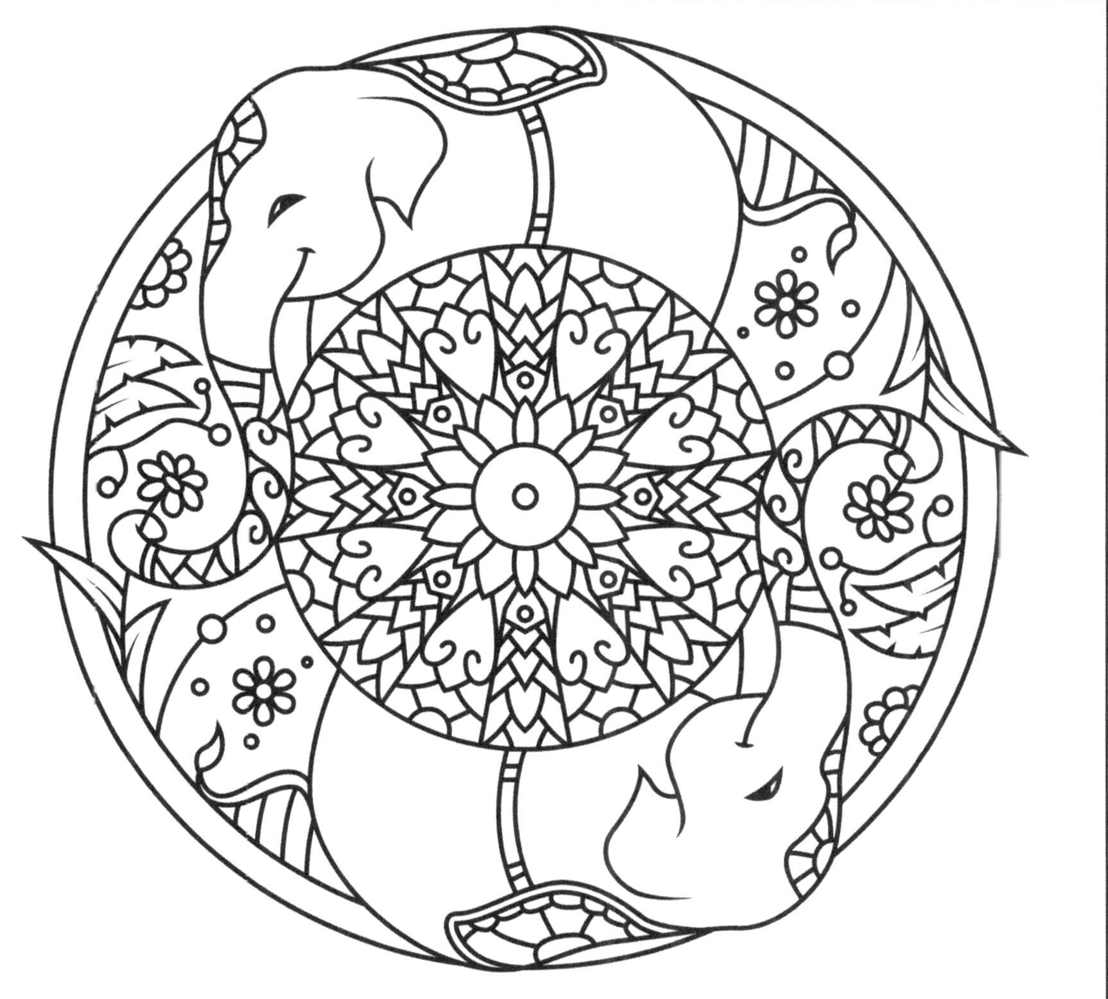

"IF YOU SEE SOMEONE WITHOUT A SMILE,
GIVE THEM ONE OF YOURS."
DOLLY PARTON

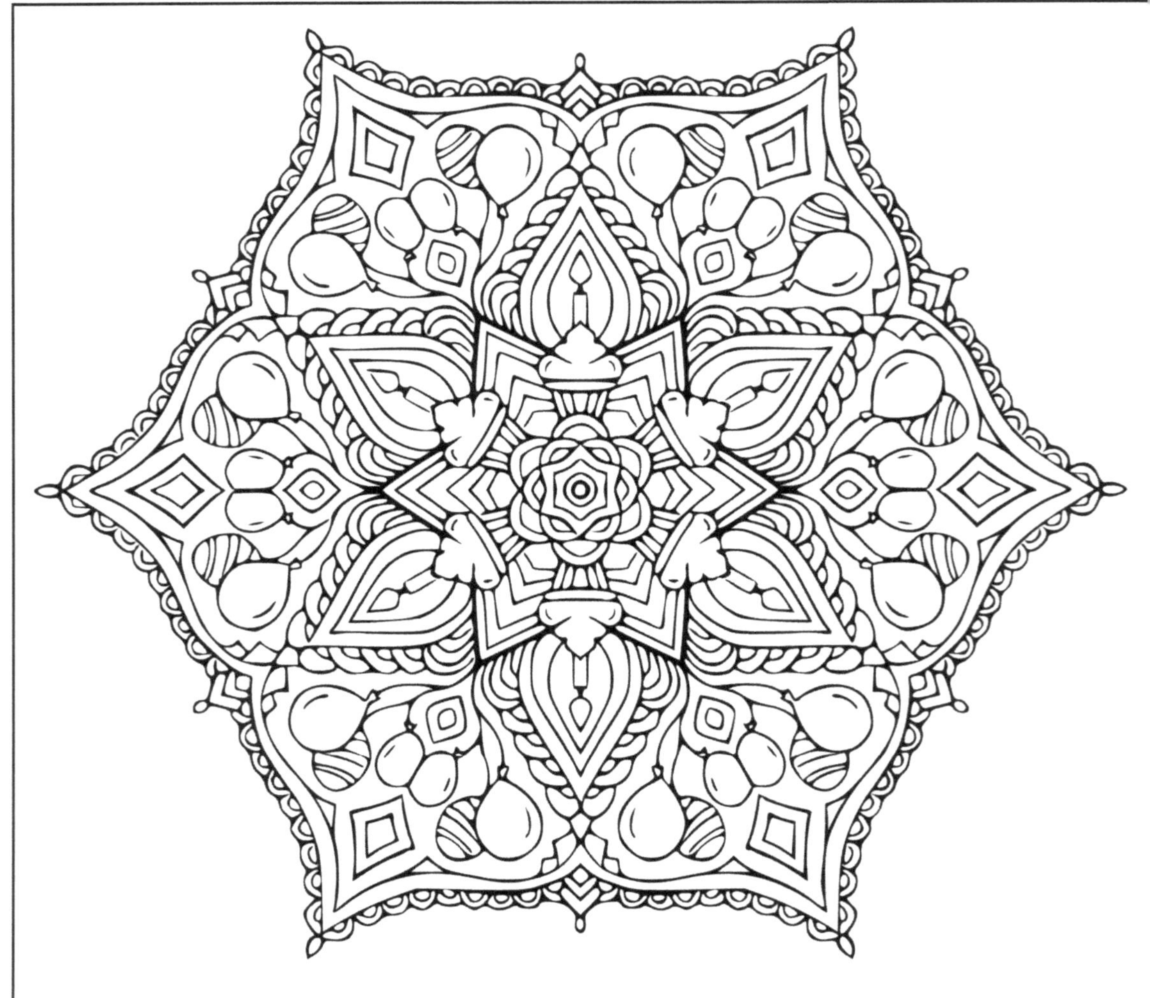

"Even though you're growing up,
you should never stop having fun."
Nina Dobrev

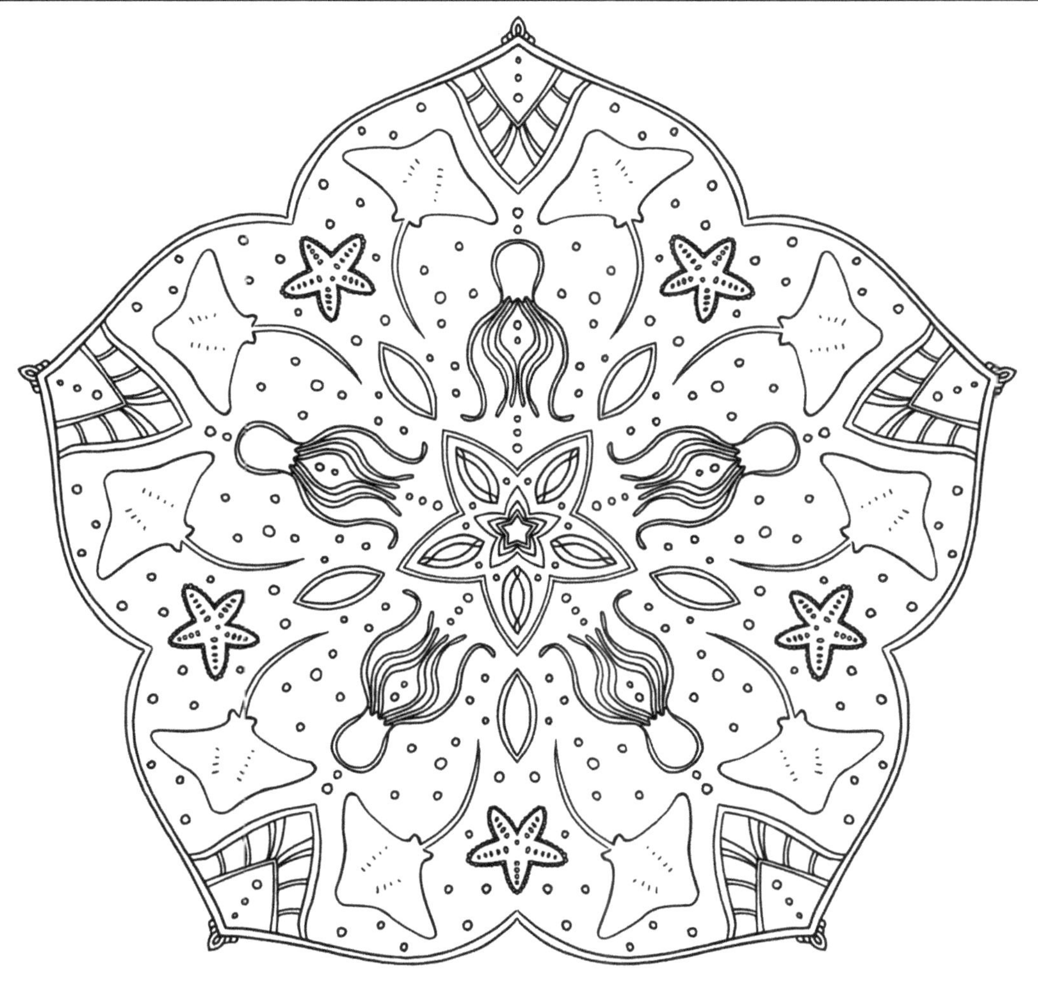

"ALWAYS BE A FIRST-RATE VERSION OF YOURSELF
INSTEAD OF A SECOND-RATE VERSION OF SOMEBODY ELSE."
JUDY GARLAND

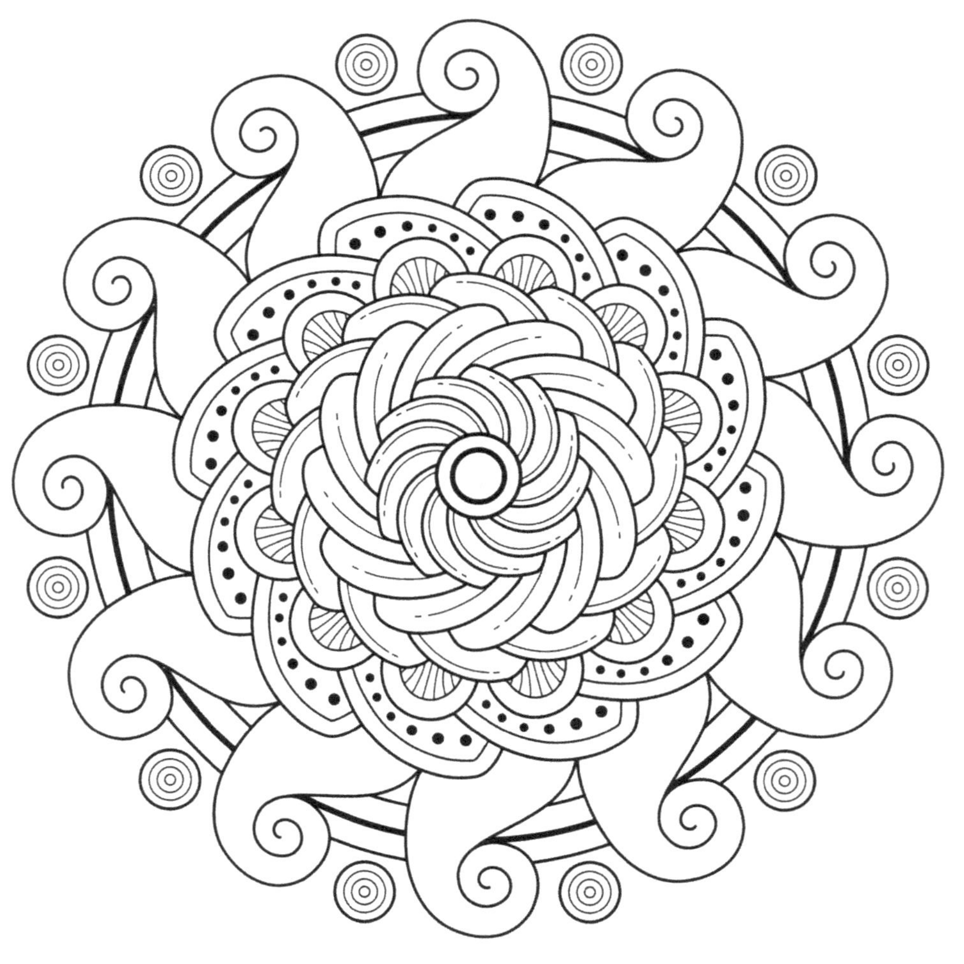

"FALL SEVEN TIMES, STAND UP EIGHT."
JAPANESE PROVERB

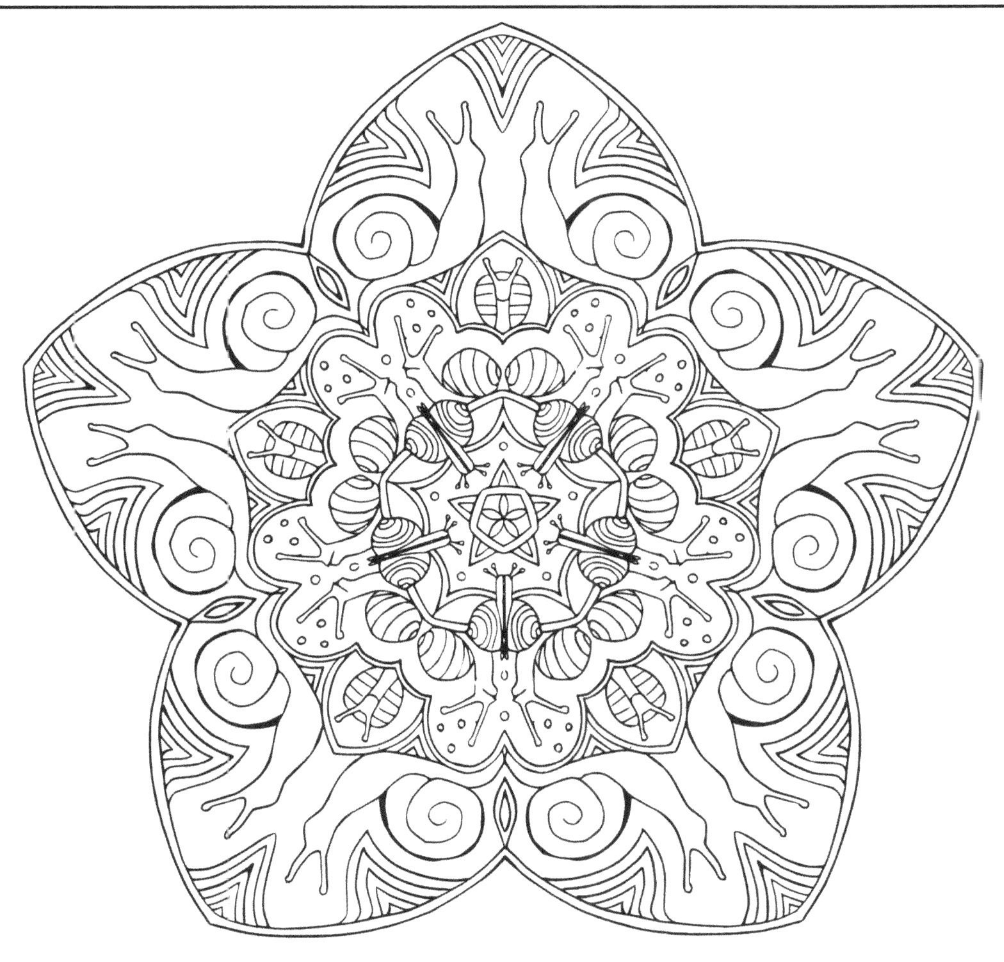

"Heroes are made by the path they choose,
not the powers they are graced with."
Iron Man

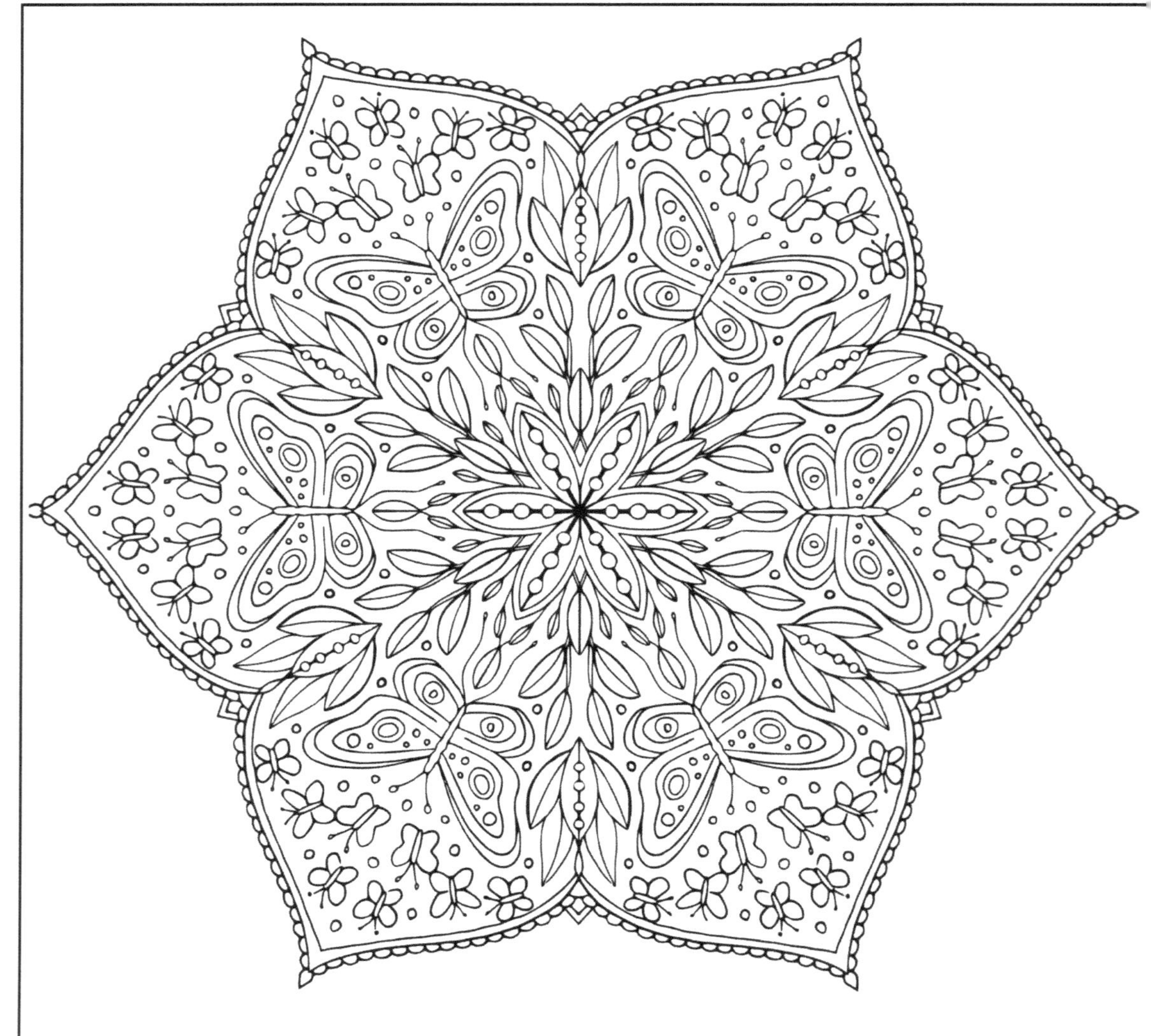

"THE BEST WAY TO PREDICT THE FUTURE IS TO CREATE IT."
ABRAHAM LINCOLN

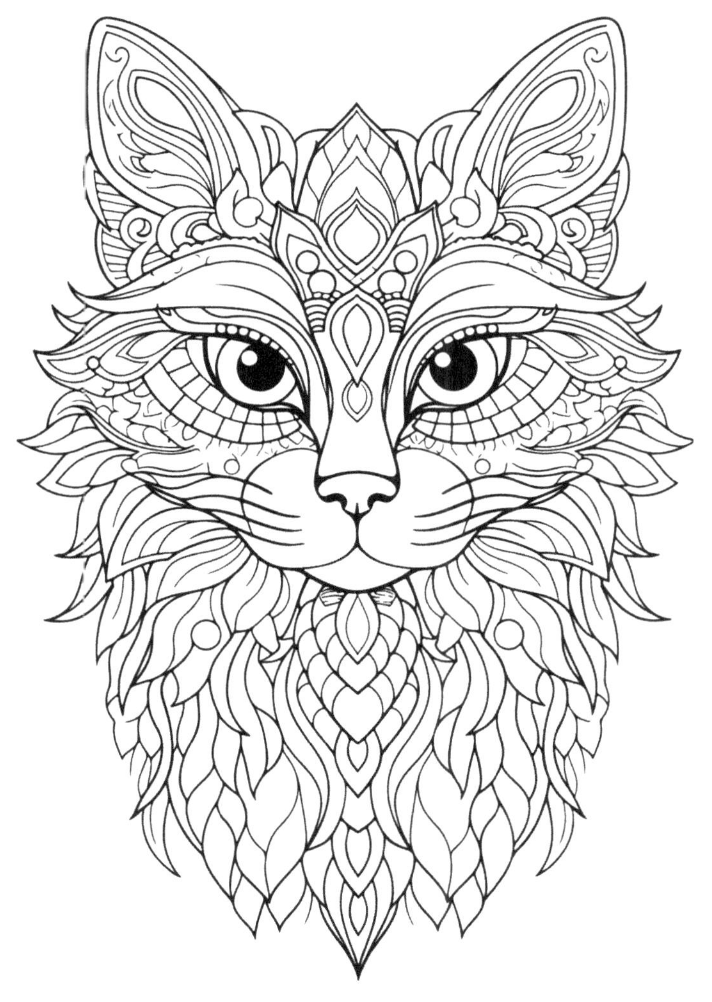

"NEVER LET THE FEAR OF STRIKING OUT
STOP YOU FROM PLAYING THE GAME."
BABE RUTH

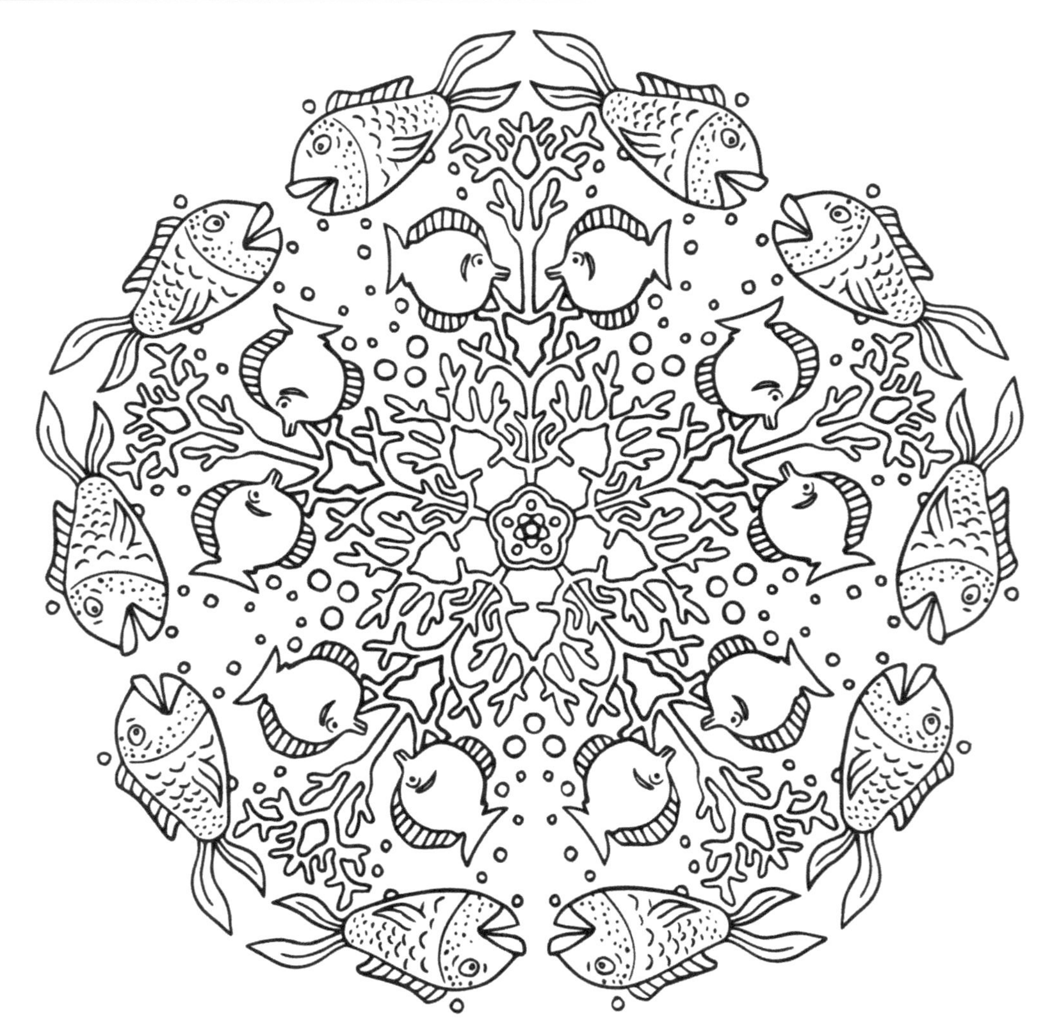

"YOU MUST BE THE CHANGE YOU WISH TO SEE IN THE WORLD."
MAHATMA GANDHI

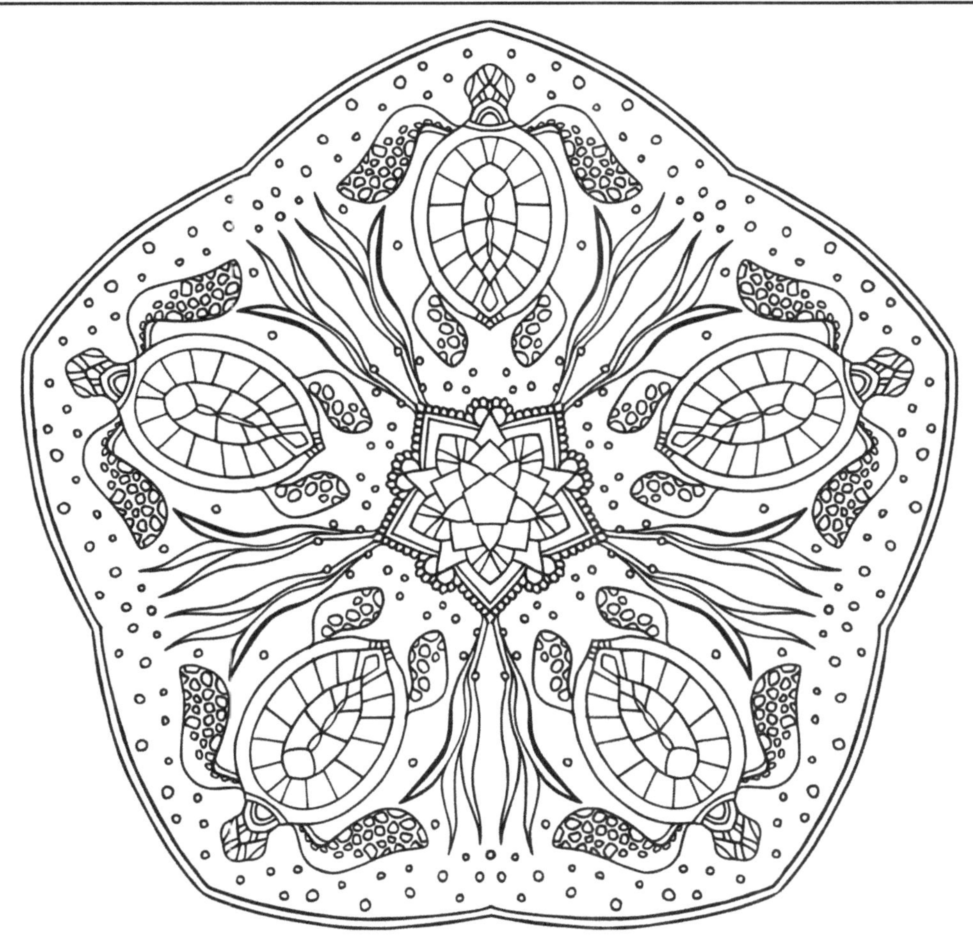

"THE CAPACITY TO LEARN IS A GIFT;
THE ABILITY TO LEARN IS A SKILL;
THE WILLINGNESS TO LEARN IS A CHOICE."
BRIAN HERBERT

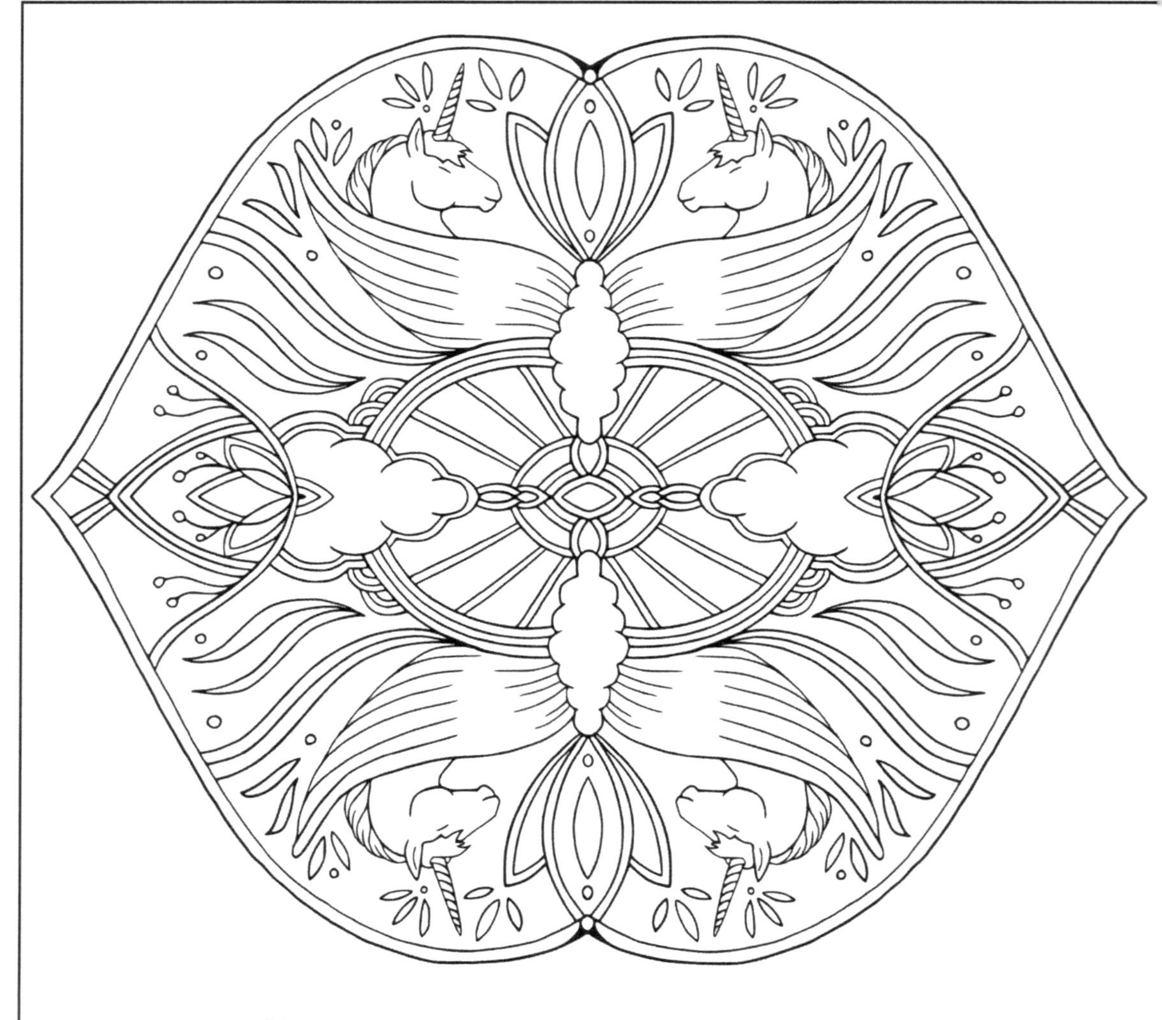

"ANYONE WHO HAS NEVER MADE A MISTAKE
HAS NEVER TRIED ANYTHING NEW."
ALBERT EINSTEIN

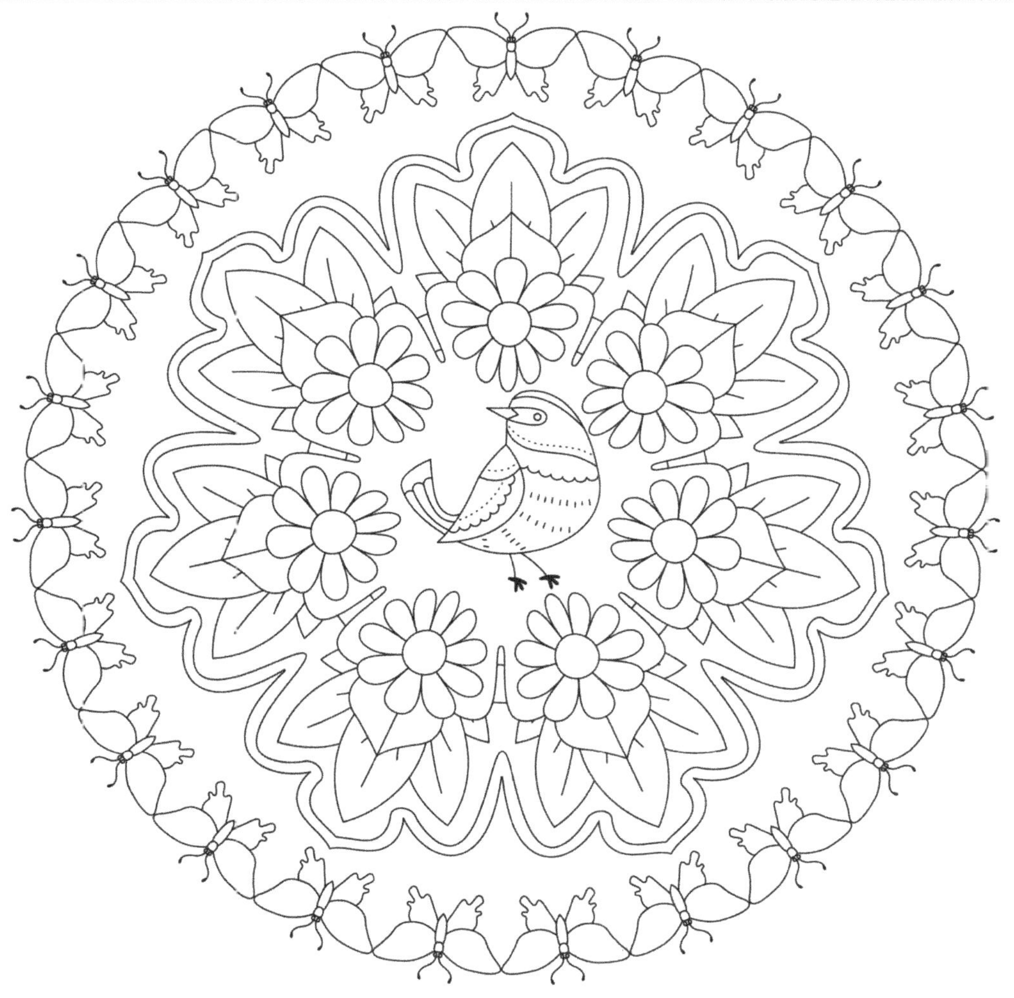

"WHEN YOU DECIDE NOT TO BE AFRAID, YOU CAN FIND FRIENDS
IN SUPER UNEXPECTED PLACES."
MS. MARVEL

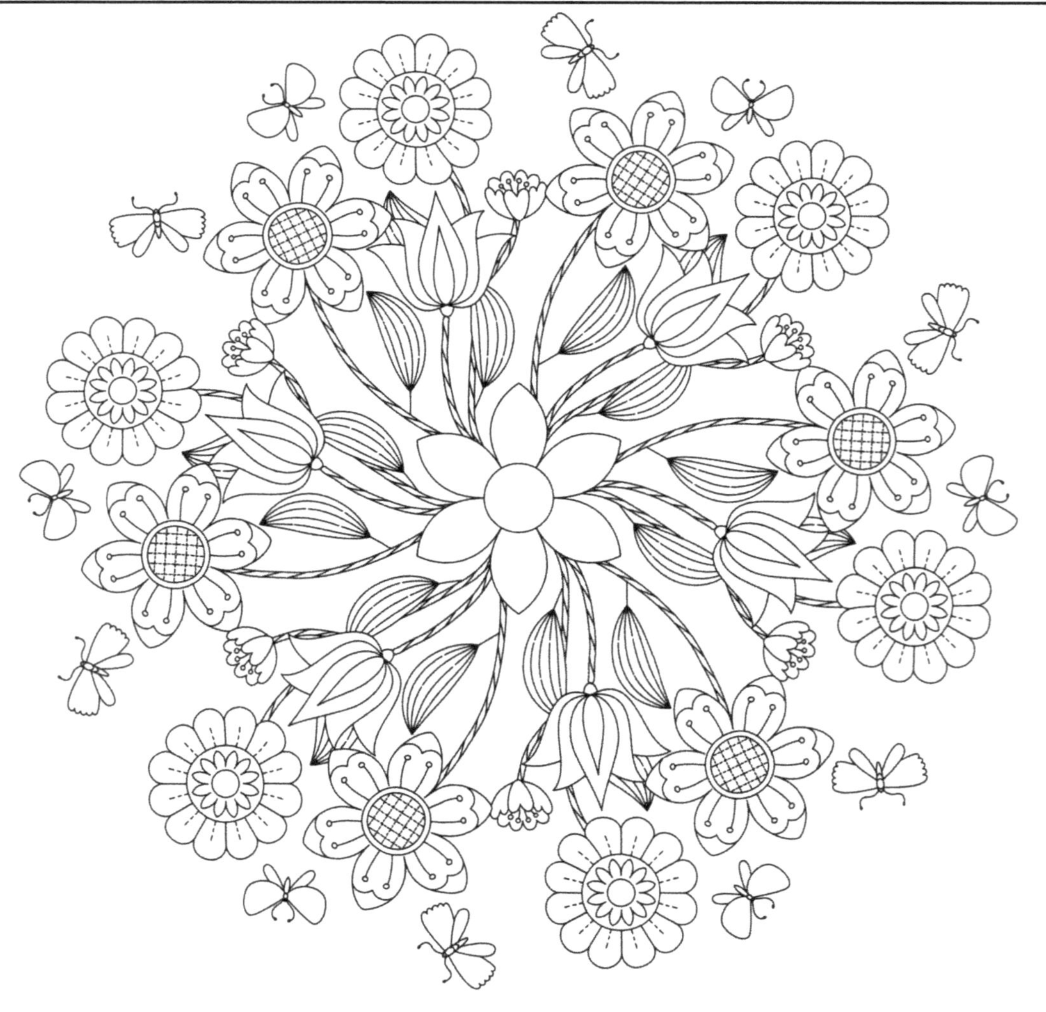

"A LITTLE CONSIDERATION, A LITTLE THOUGHT FOR OTHERS,
MAKES ALL THE DIFFERENCE."
EEYORE, WINNIE-THE-POOH

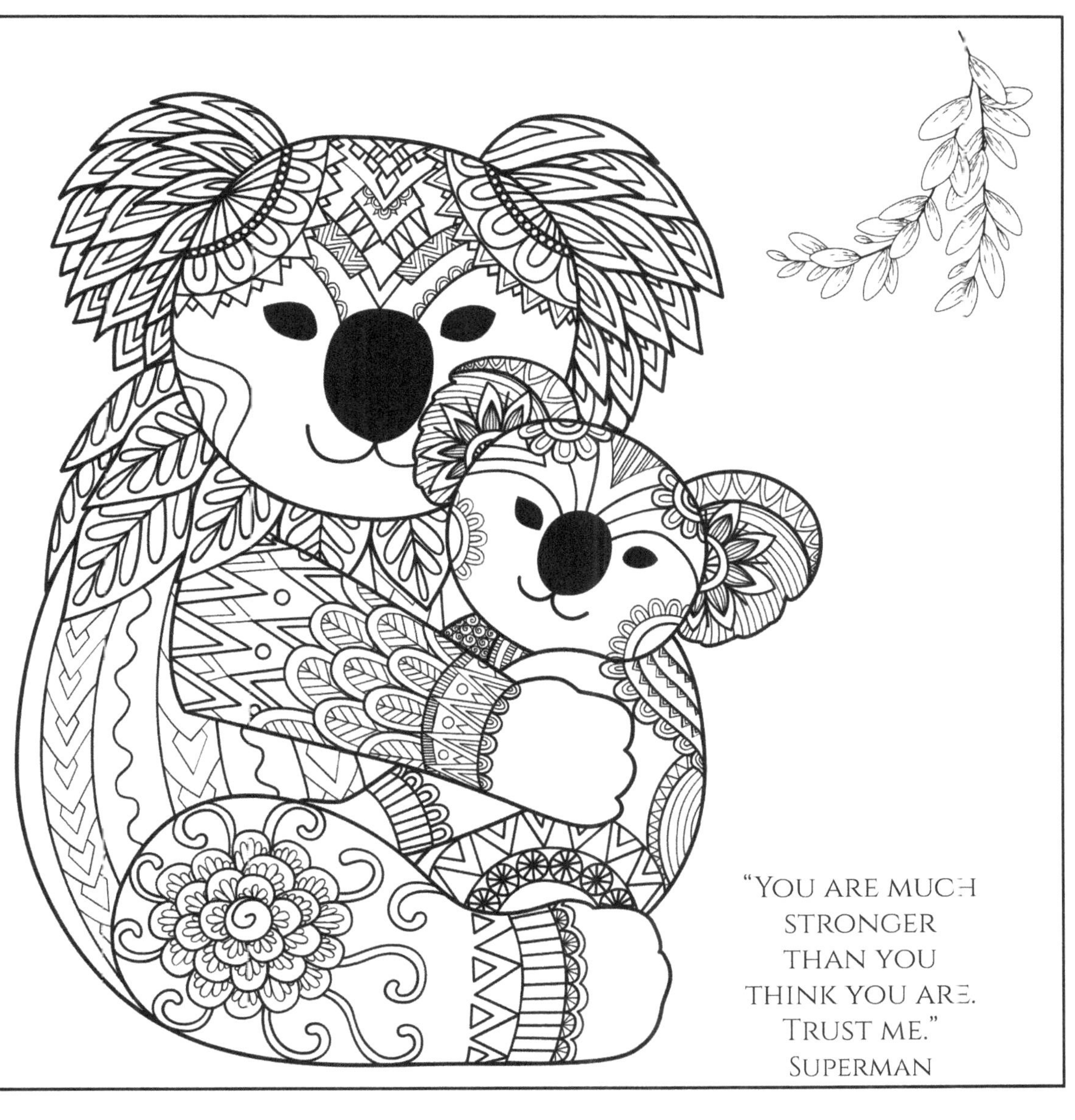

"YOU ARE MUCH
STRONGER
THAN YOU
THINK YOU ARE.
TRUST ME."
SUPERMAN

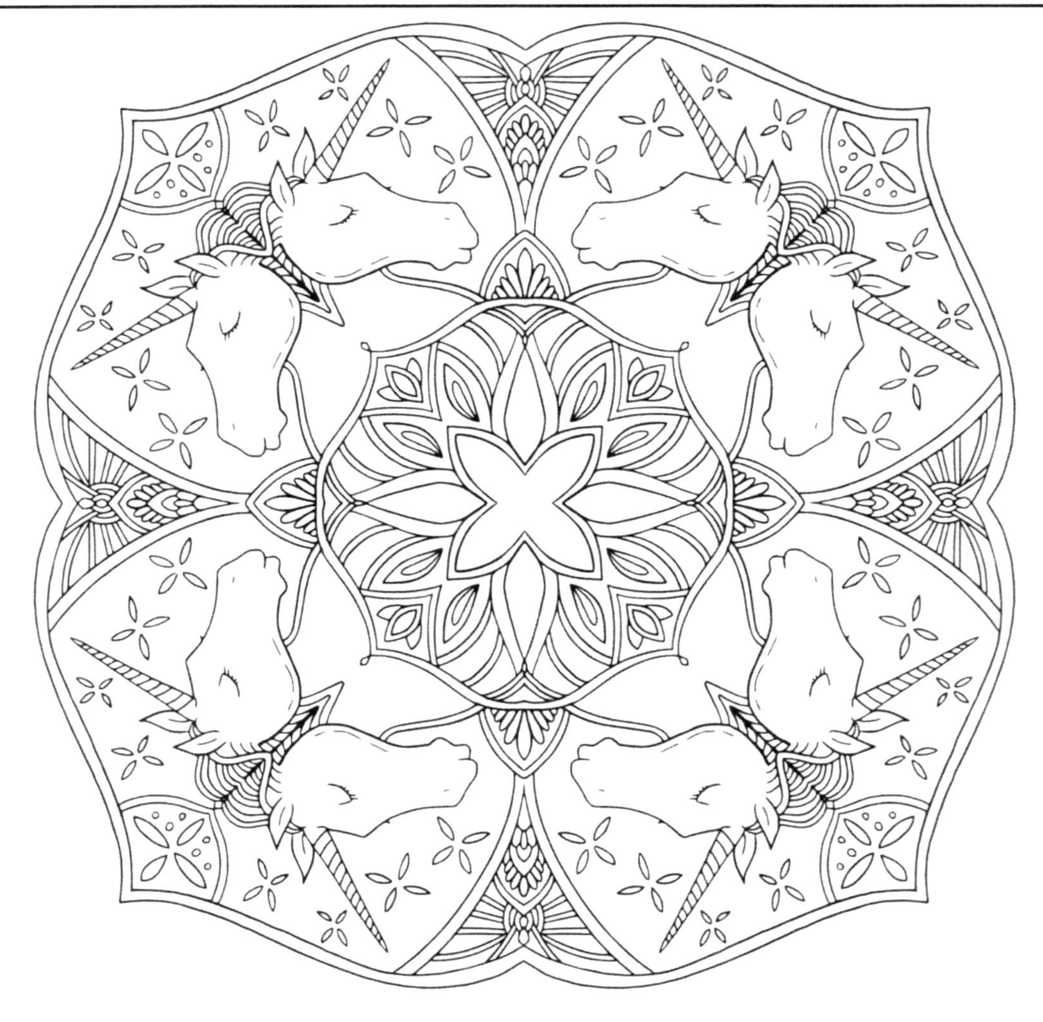

"BE SO GOOD THEY CAN'T IGNORE YOU."
STEVE MARTIN

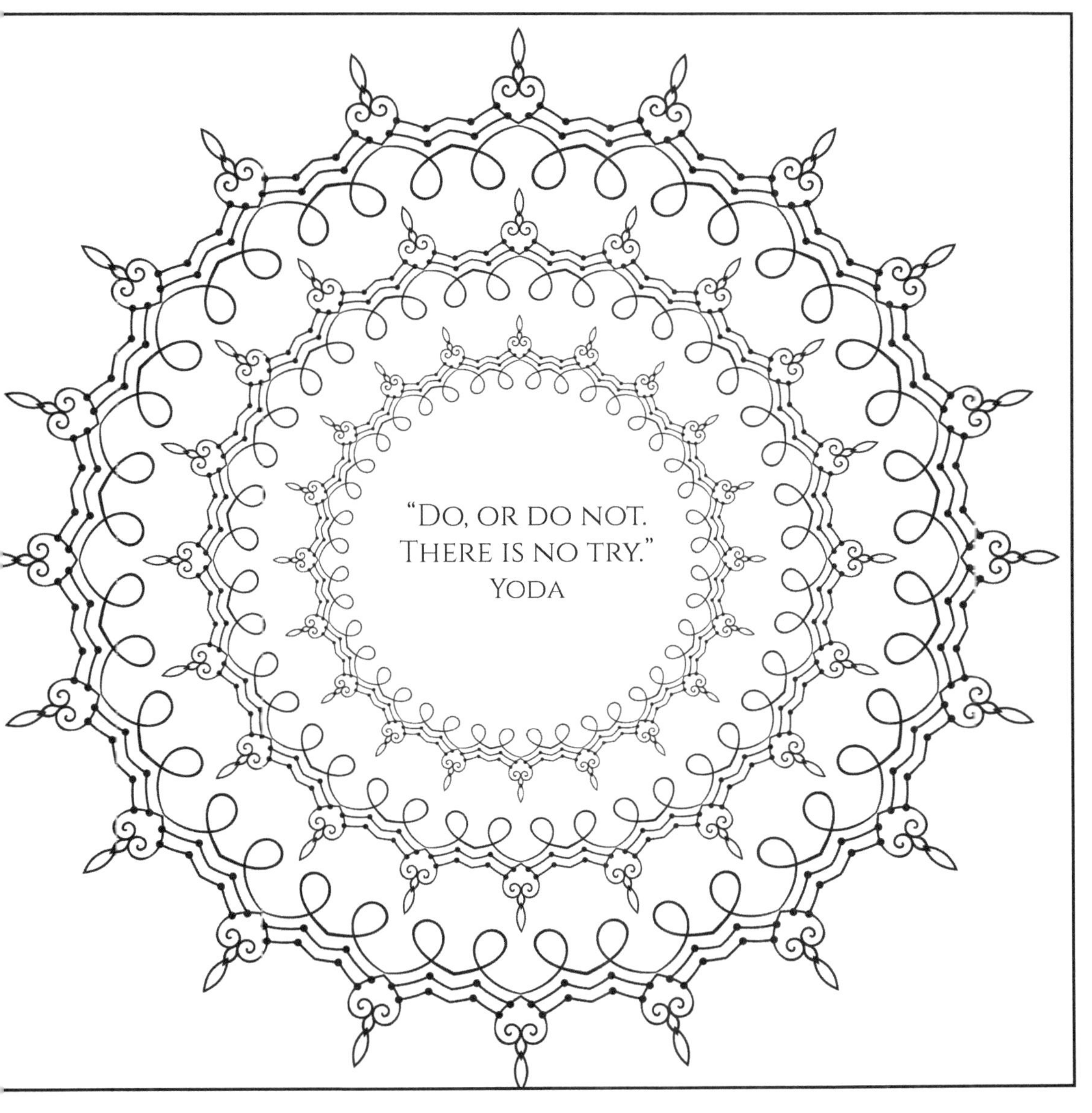
"DO, OR DO NOT.
THERE IS NO TRY."
YODA

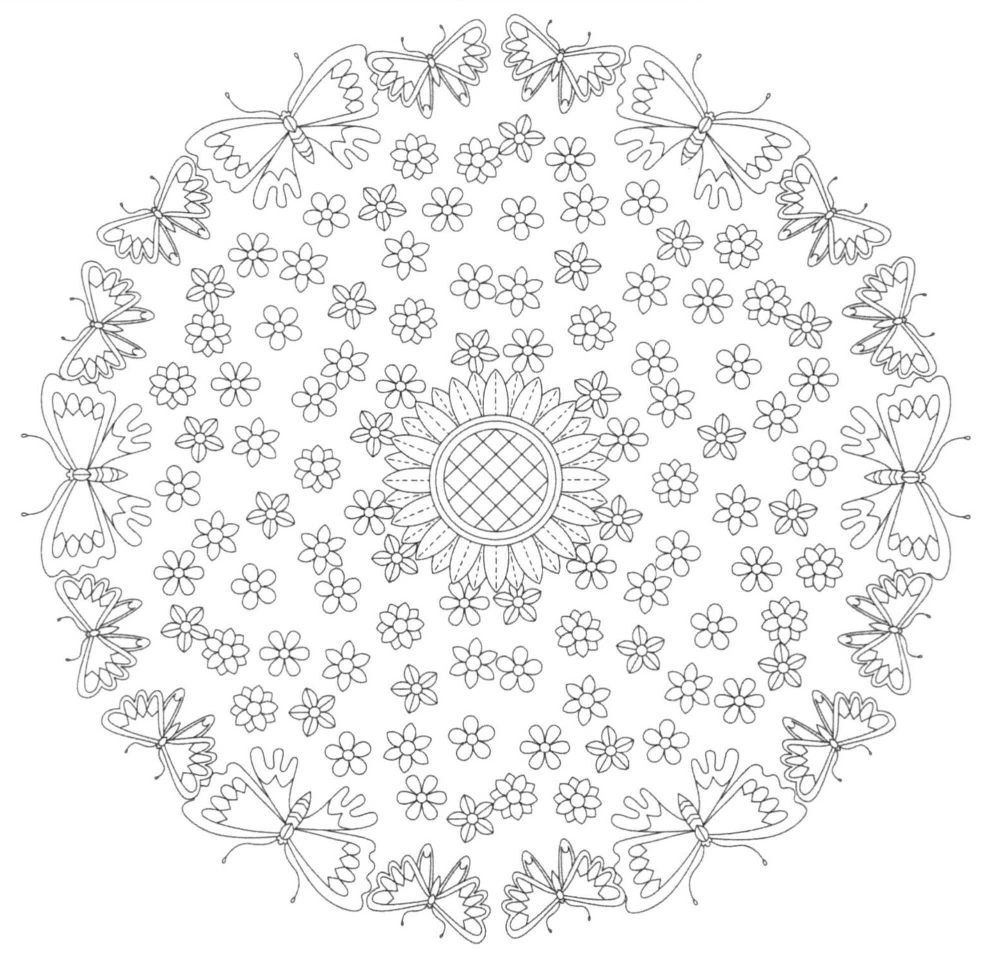

"GOOD FRIENDS HELP YOU TO FIND IMPORTANT THINGS
WHEN YOU HAVE LOST THEM . . .
YOUR SMILE, YOUR HOPE, AND YOUR COURAGE."
DOE ZANTAMATA

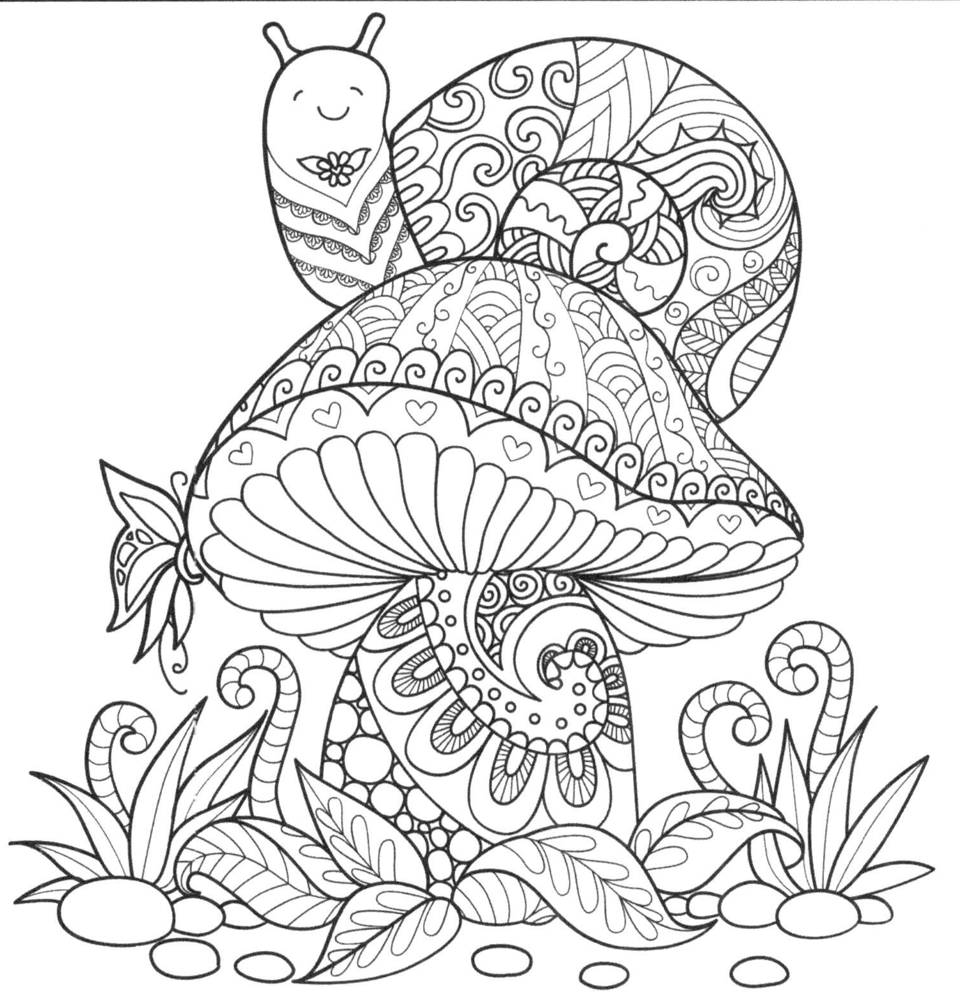

"DON'T LET WHAT YOU CAN'T DO STOP YOU
FROM DOING WHAT YOU CAN DO."
JOHN WOODEN

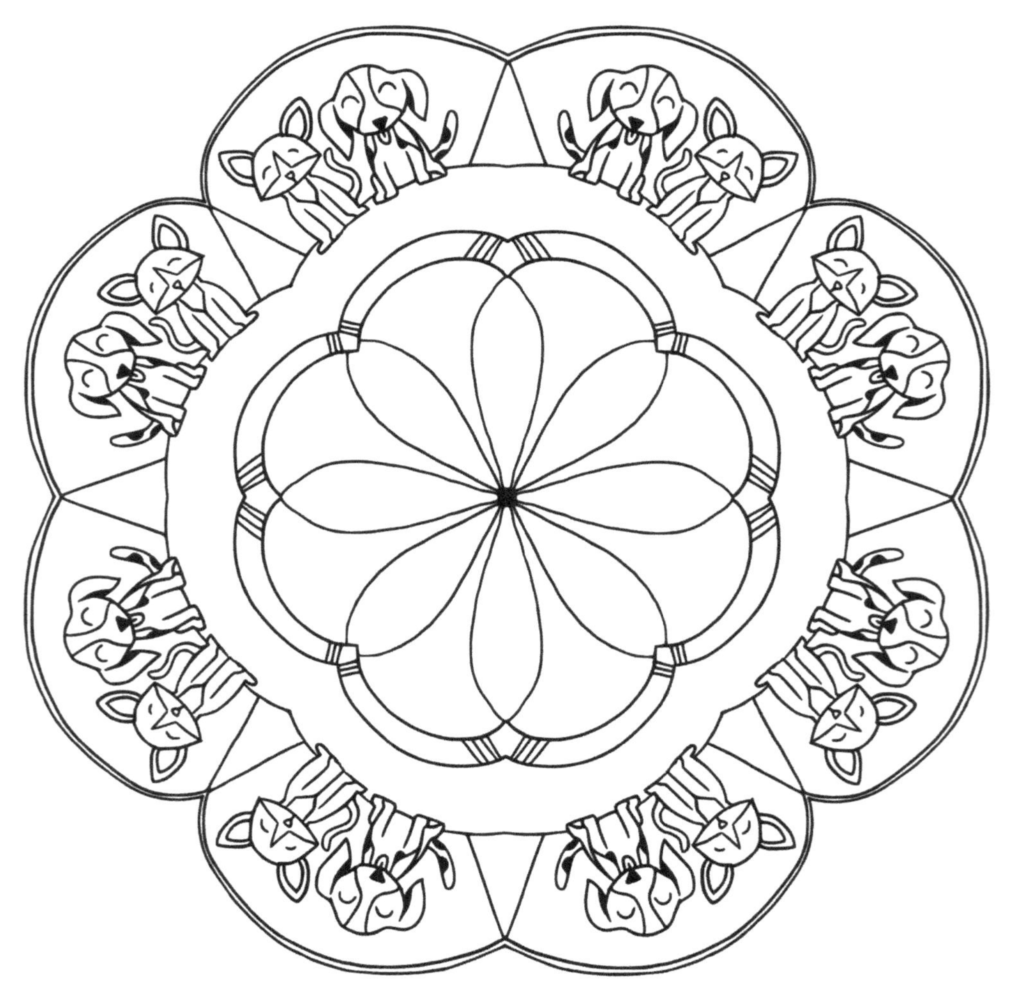

"A FRIEND IS SOMEONE WHO KNOWS ALL ABOUT YOU
AND STILL LOVES YOU."
ELBERT HUBBARD

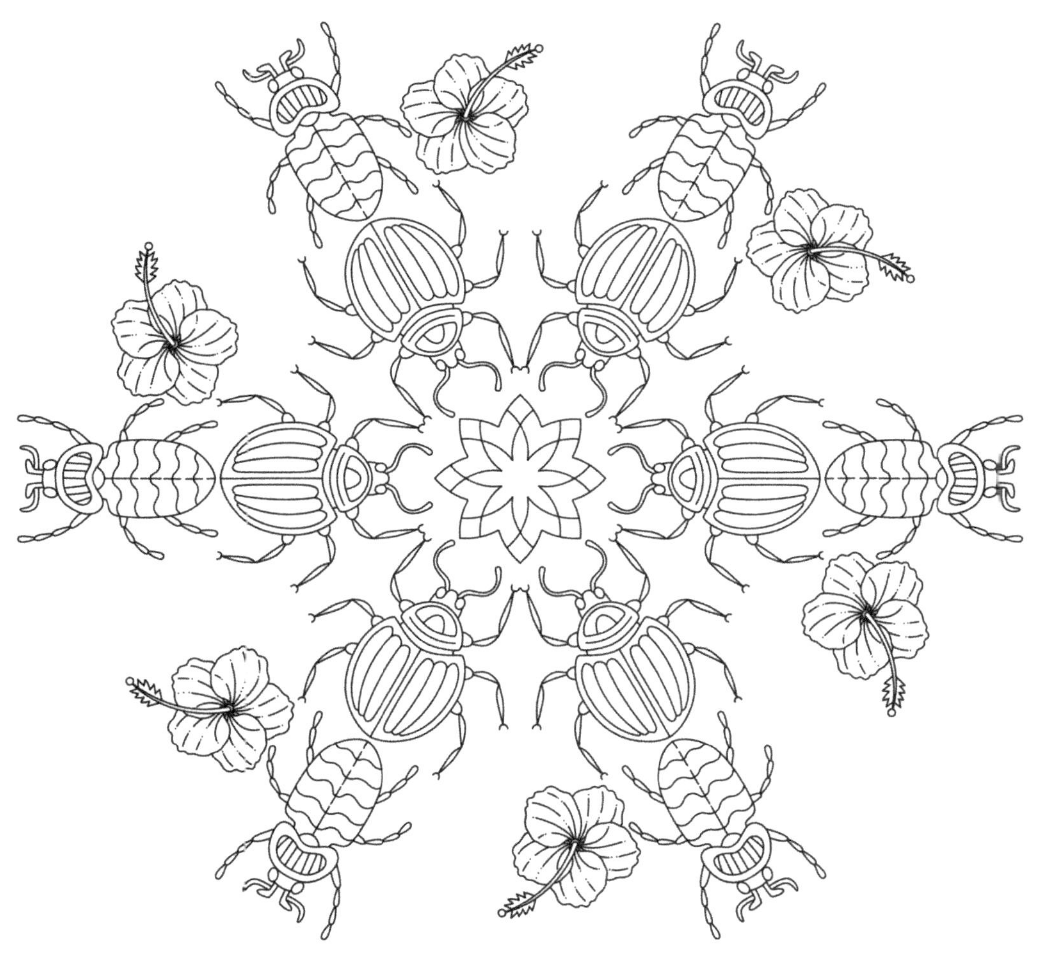

"NEVER LET THE ODDS KEEP YOU FROM DOING
WHAT YOU KNOW IN YOUR HEART
YOU WERE MEANT TO DO."
H. JACKSON BROWN

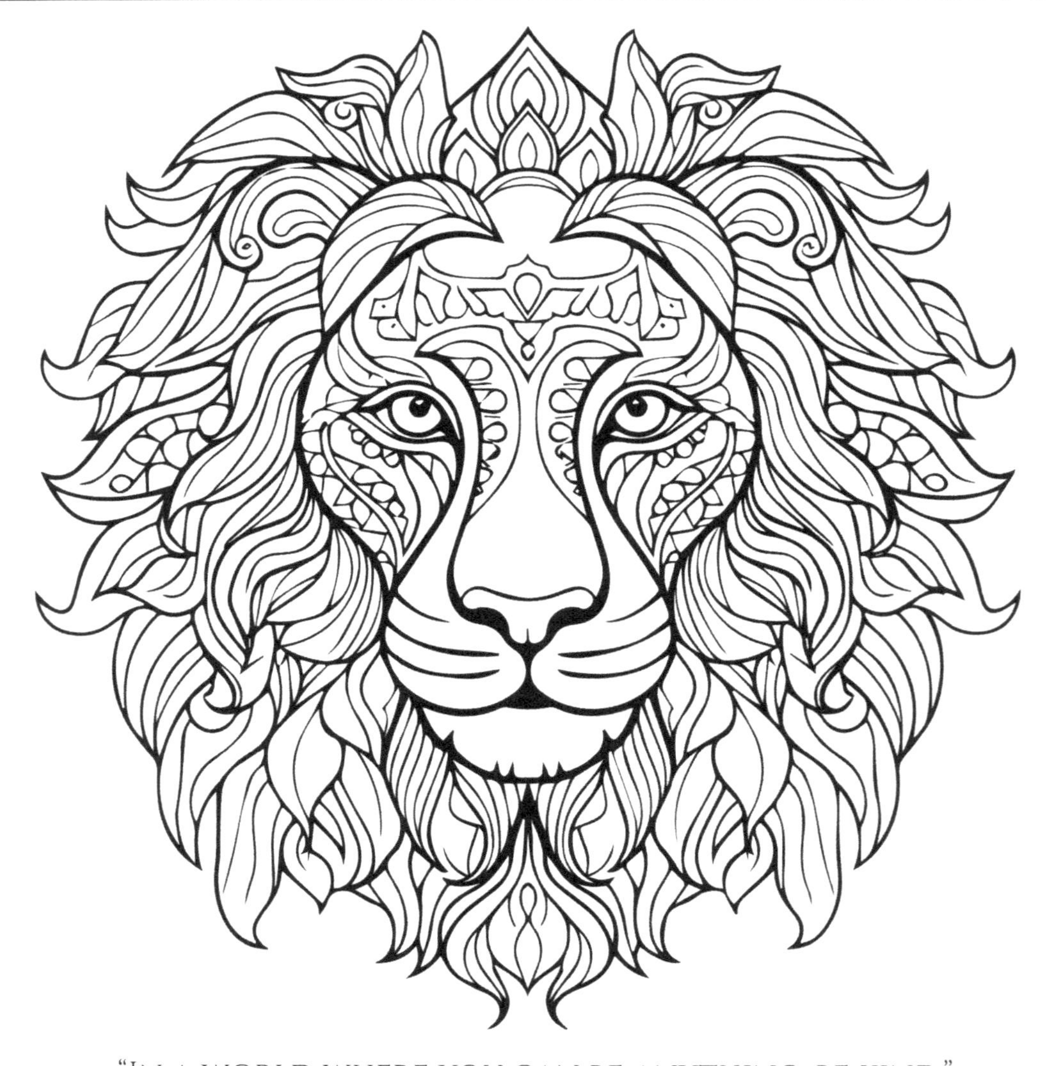

"IN A WORLD WHERE YOU CAN BE ANYTHING, BE KIND."
JENNIFER DUKES LEE

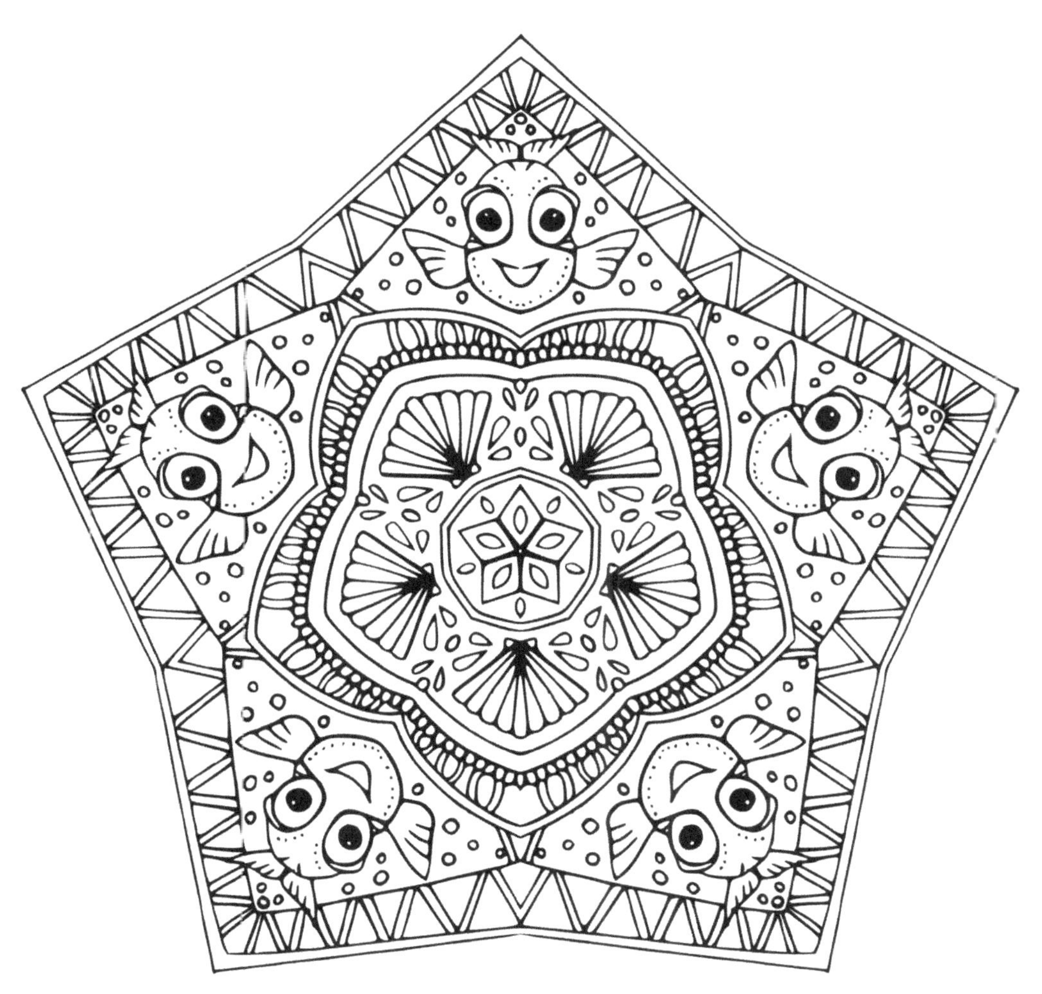

"IT'S NOT WHAT HAPPENS TO YOU,
BUT HOW YOU REACT TO IT THAT MATTERS."
EPICTETUS

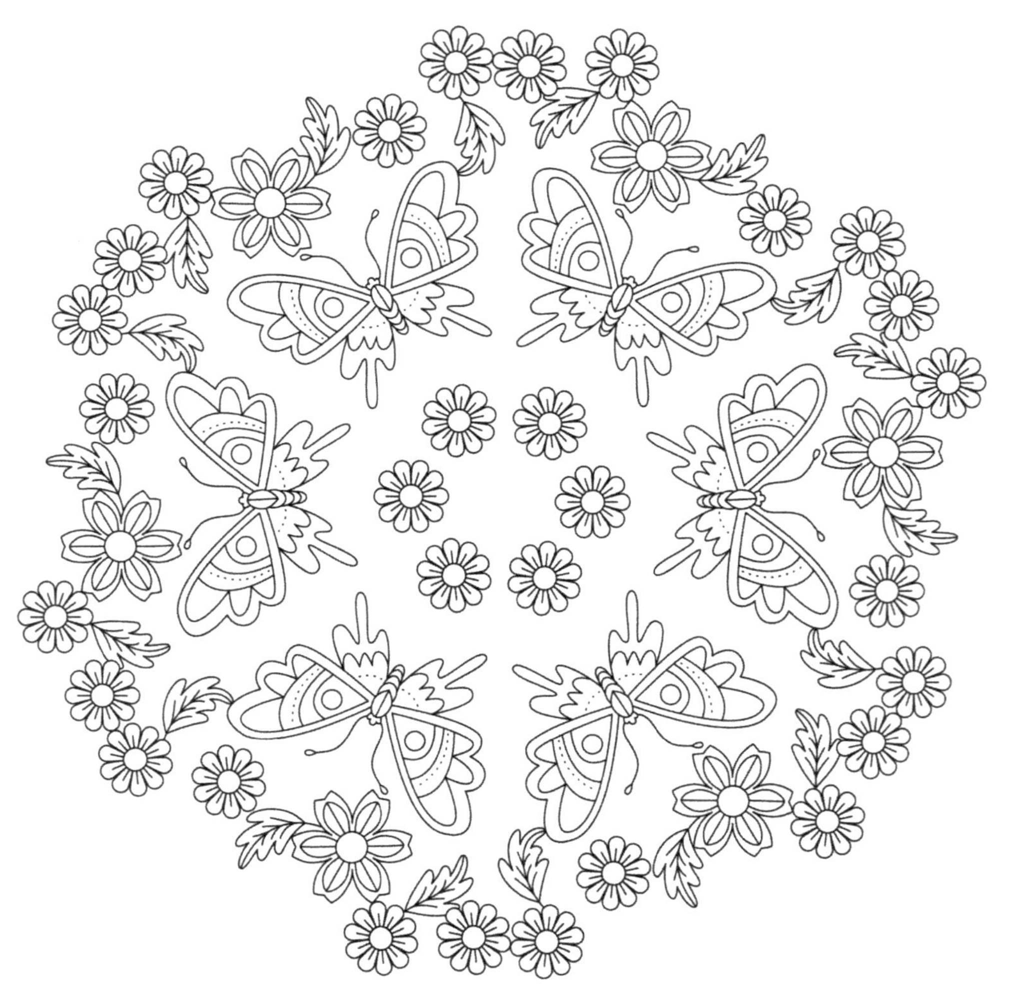

"WORK HARD, BE KIND, AND AMAZING THINGS WILL HAPPEN."
CONAN O'BRIEN

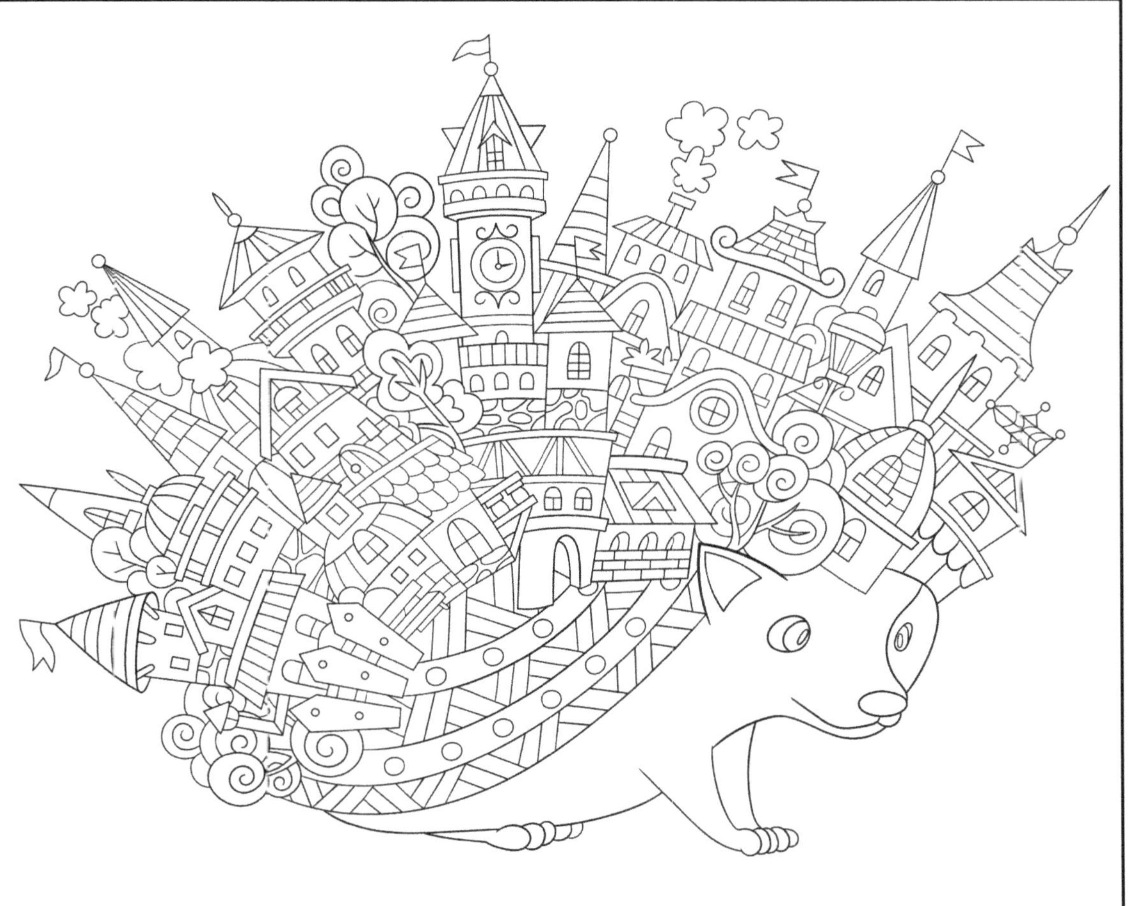

"LOGIC WILL TAKE YOU FROM A TO B.
IMAGINATION WILL TAKE YOU EVERYWHERE."
ALBERT EINSTEIN

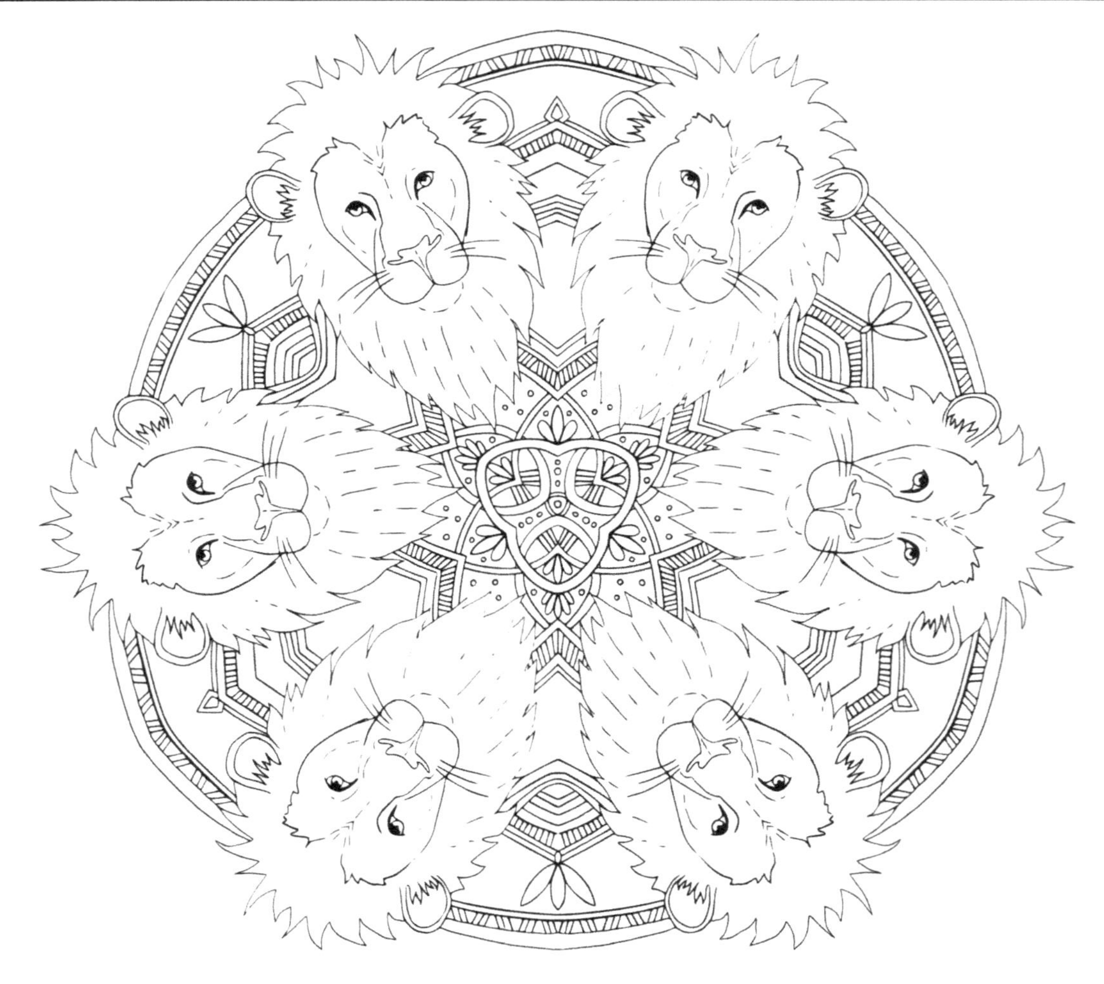

"NEVER LOOK DOWN ON ANYBODY
UNLESS YOU'RE HELPING THEM UP."
JESSE JACKSON

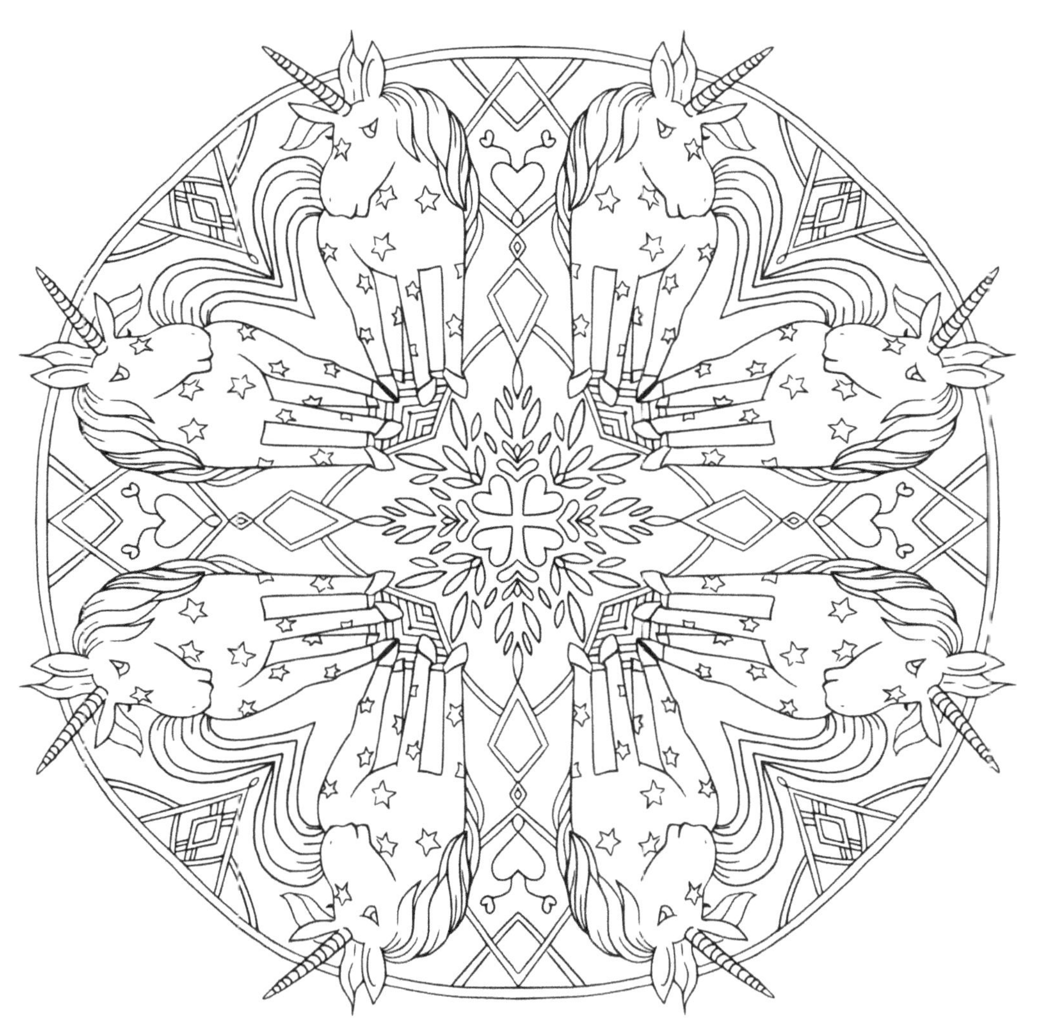

"If you can dream it, you can do it."
Walt Disney

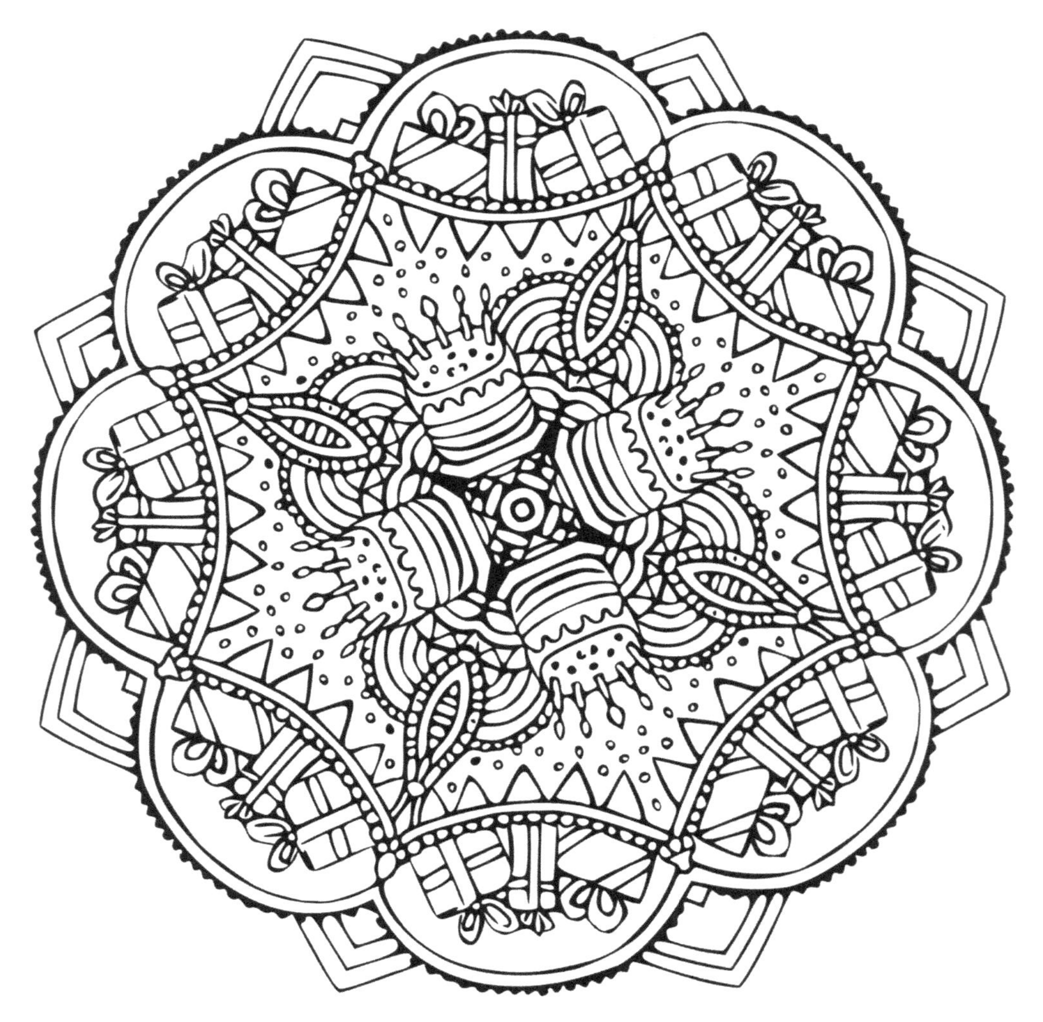

"YOU ALWAYS PASS FAILURE ON THE WAY TO SUCCESS."
MICKEY ROONEY

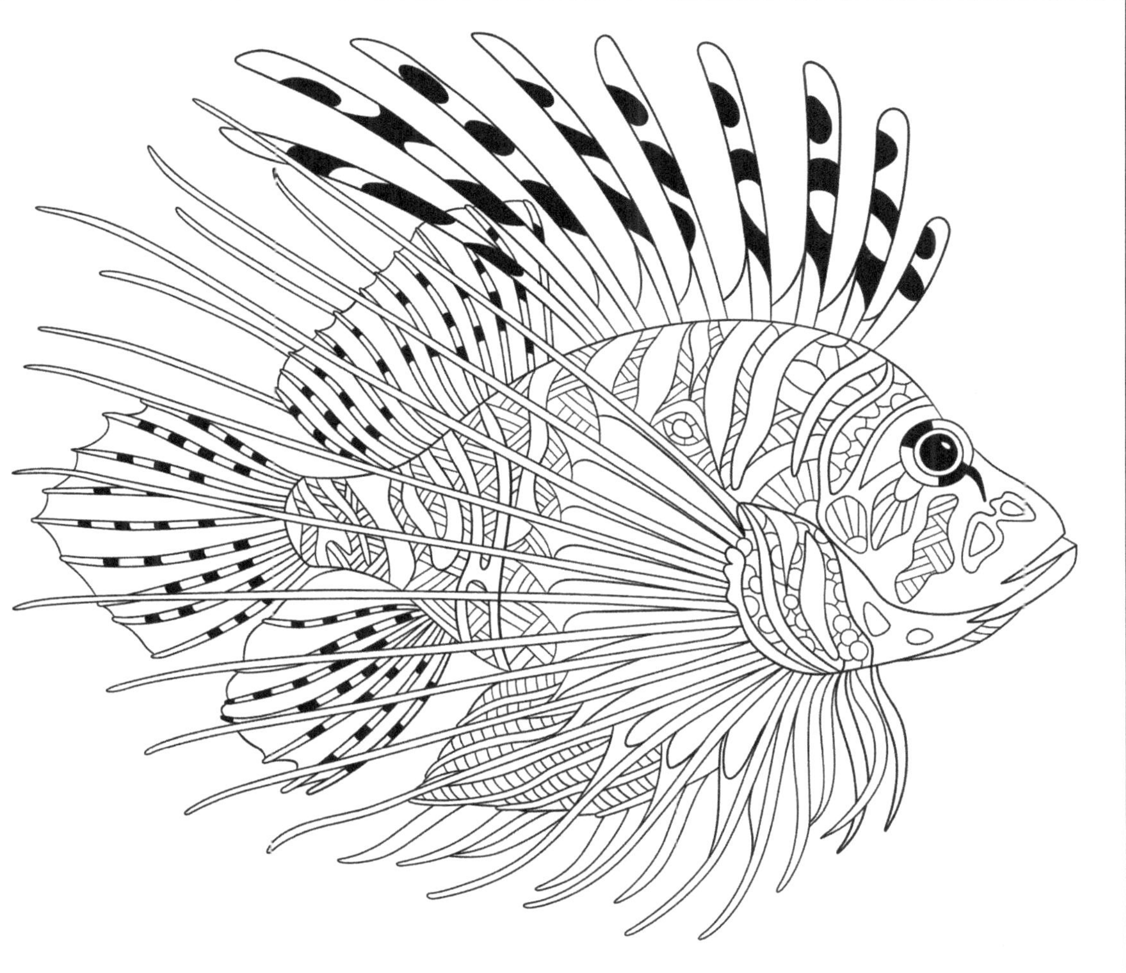

"The people who are crazy enough
to believe they can change the world
are the ones who do."
Steve Jobs

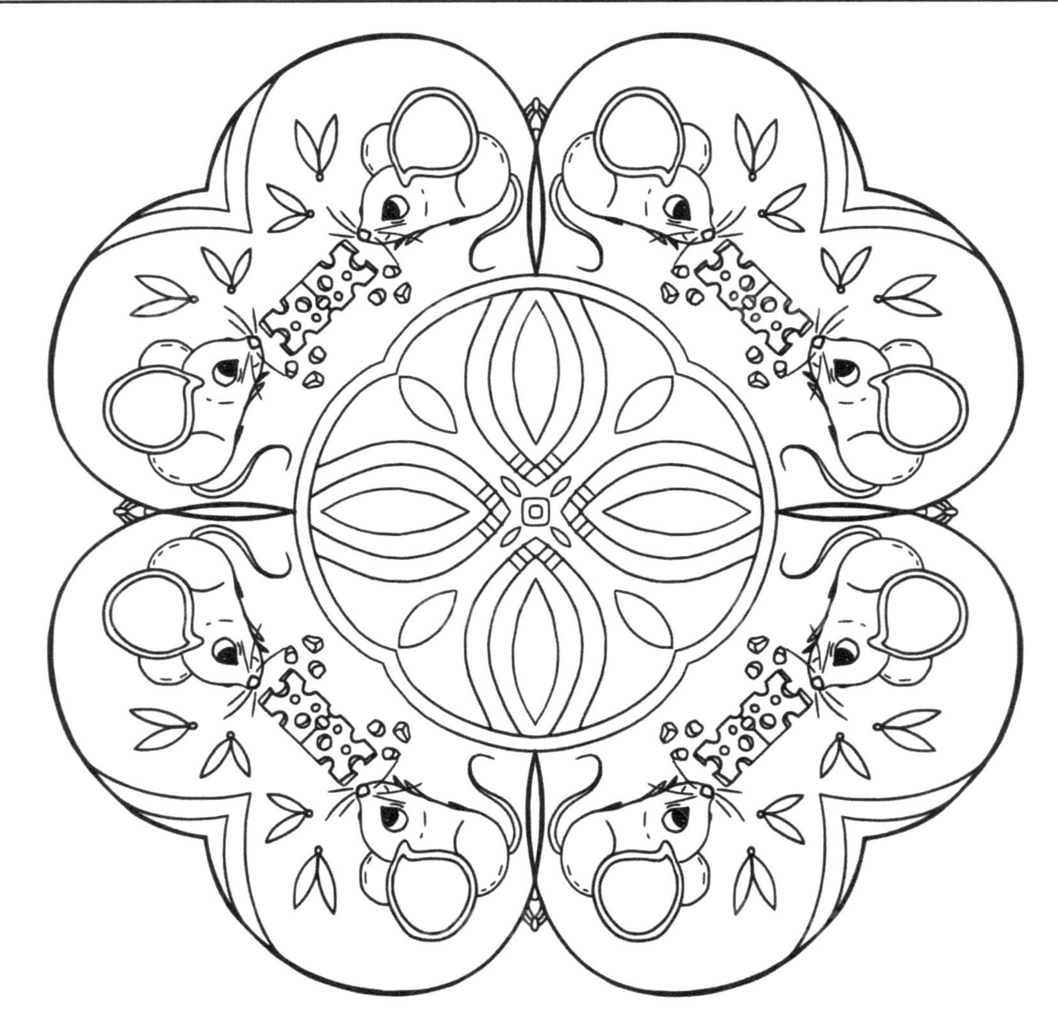

"THE TIME IS ALWAYS RIGHT TO DO WHAT IS RIGHT."
MARTIN LUTHER KING, JR.

"ONLY SURROUND YOURSELF WITH PEOPLE
WHO WILL LIFT YOU HIGHER."
OPRAH WINFREY

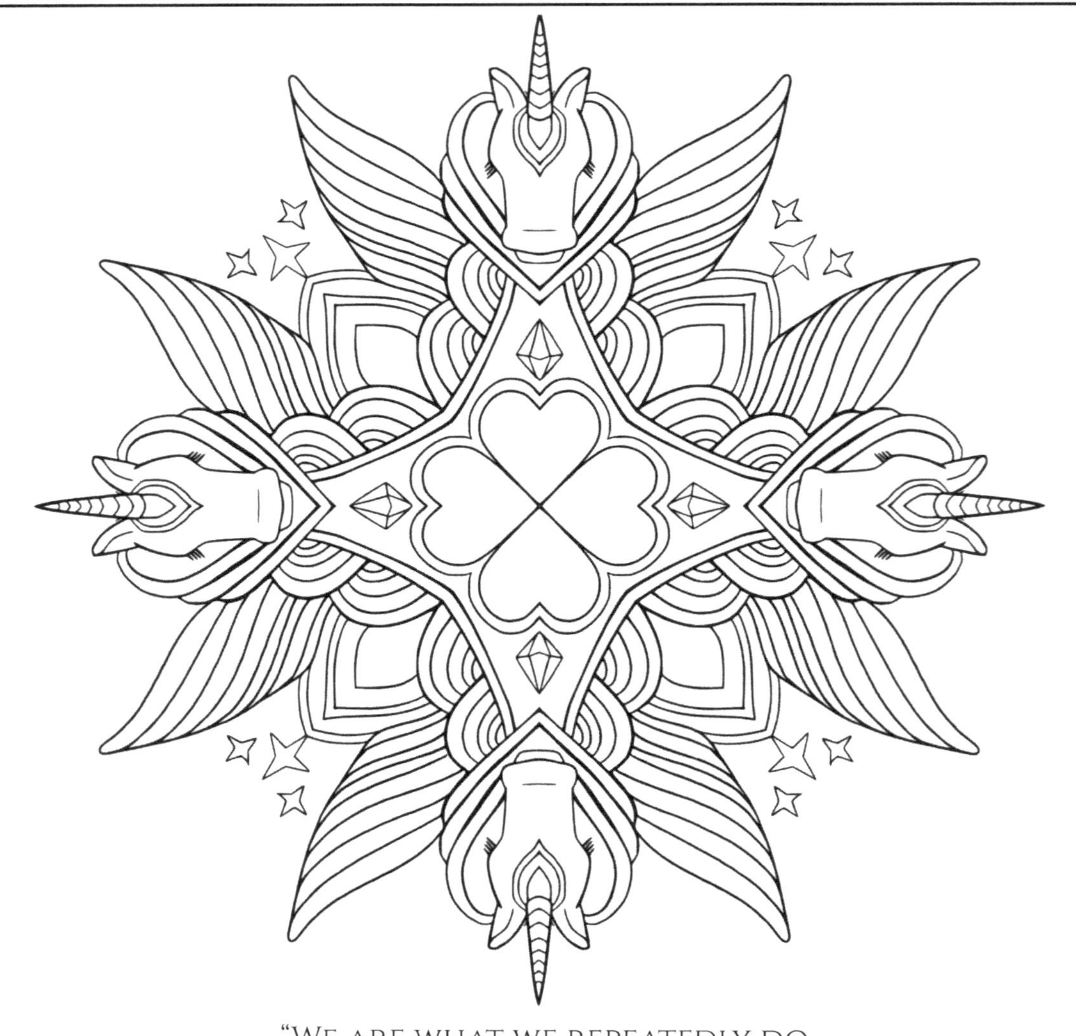

"WE ARE WHAT WE REPEATEDLY DO.
EXCELLENCE THEN, IS NOT AN ACT, BUT A HABIT."
ARISTOTLE

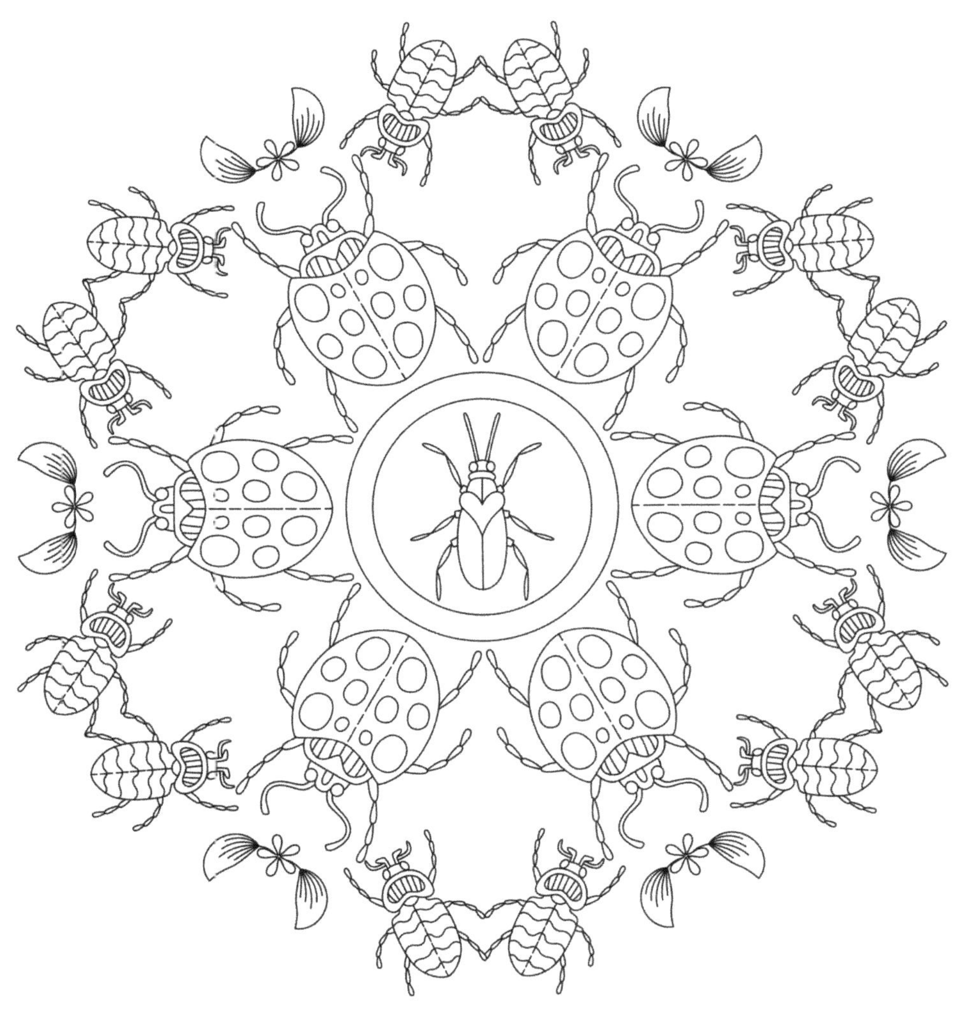

"BE KIND TO UNKIND PEOPLE. THEY NEED IT THE MOST."
ASHLEIGH BRILLIANT

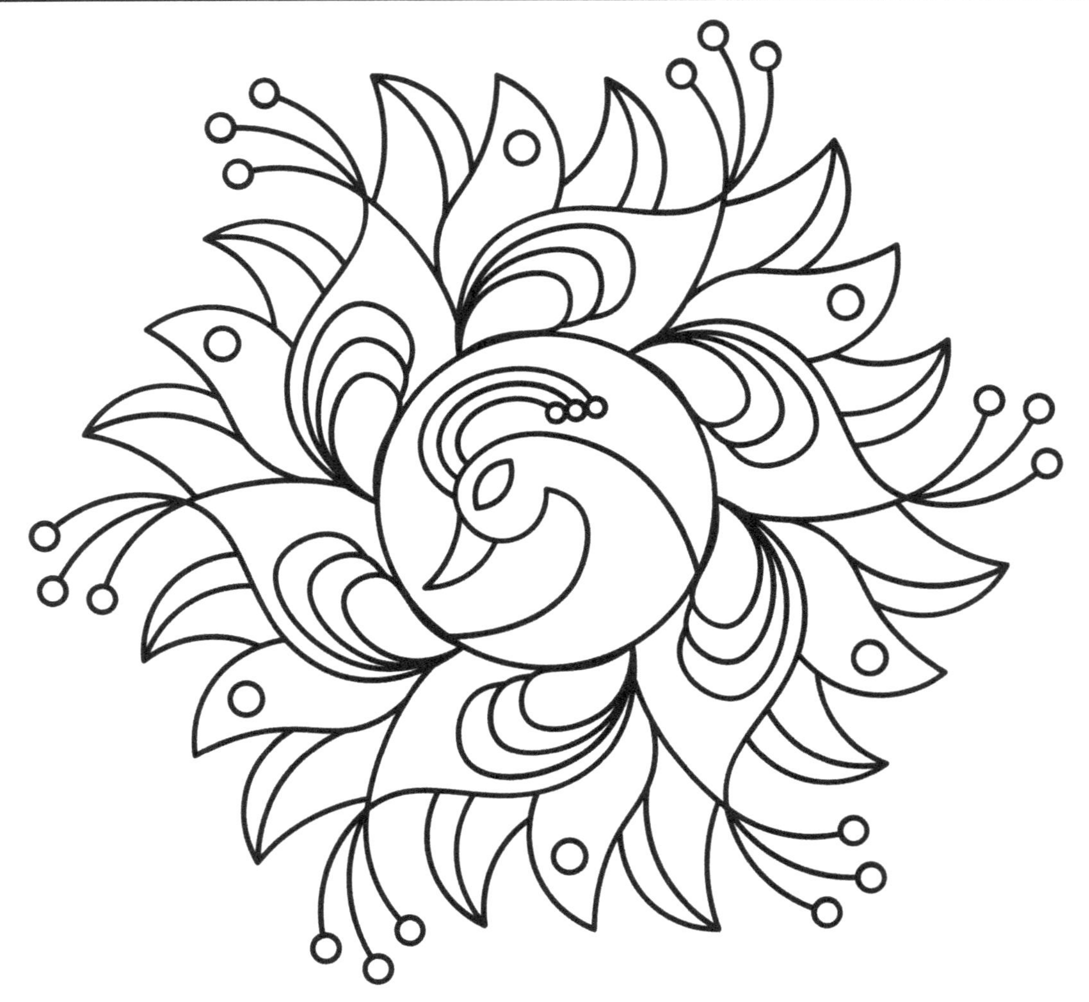

"YOU ARE ALWAYS RESPONSIBLE FOR HOW YOU ACT,
NO MATTER HOW YOU FEEL."
ROBERT TEW

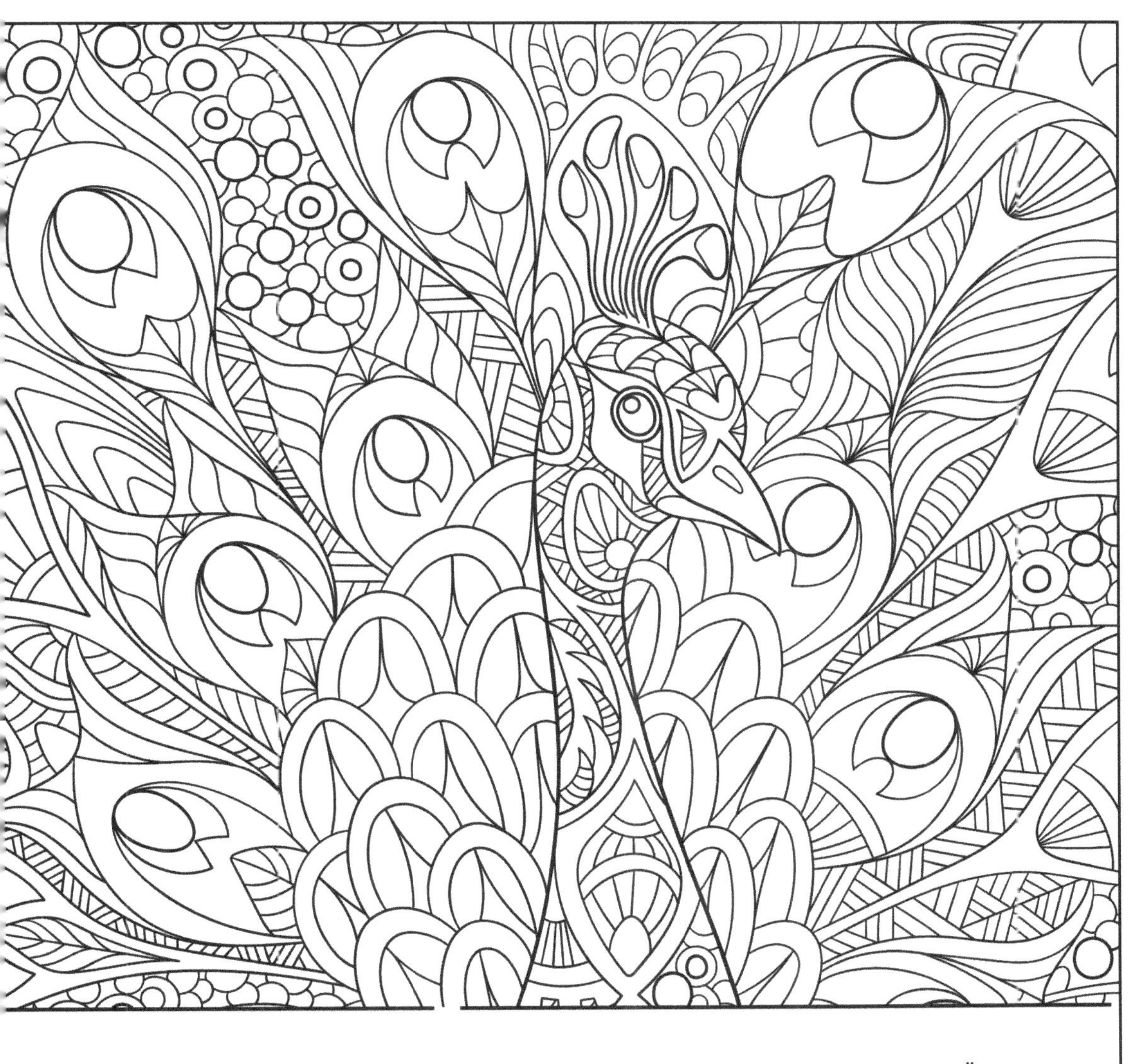

"LIFE DOESN'T GIVE US PURPOSE. WE GIVE LIFE PURPOSE."
THE FLASH

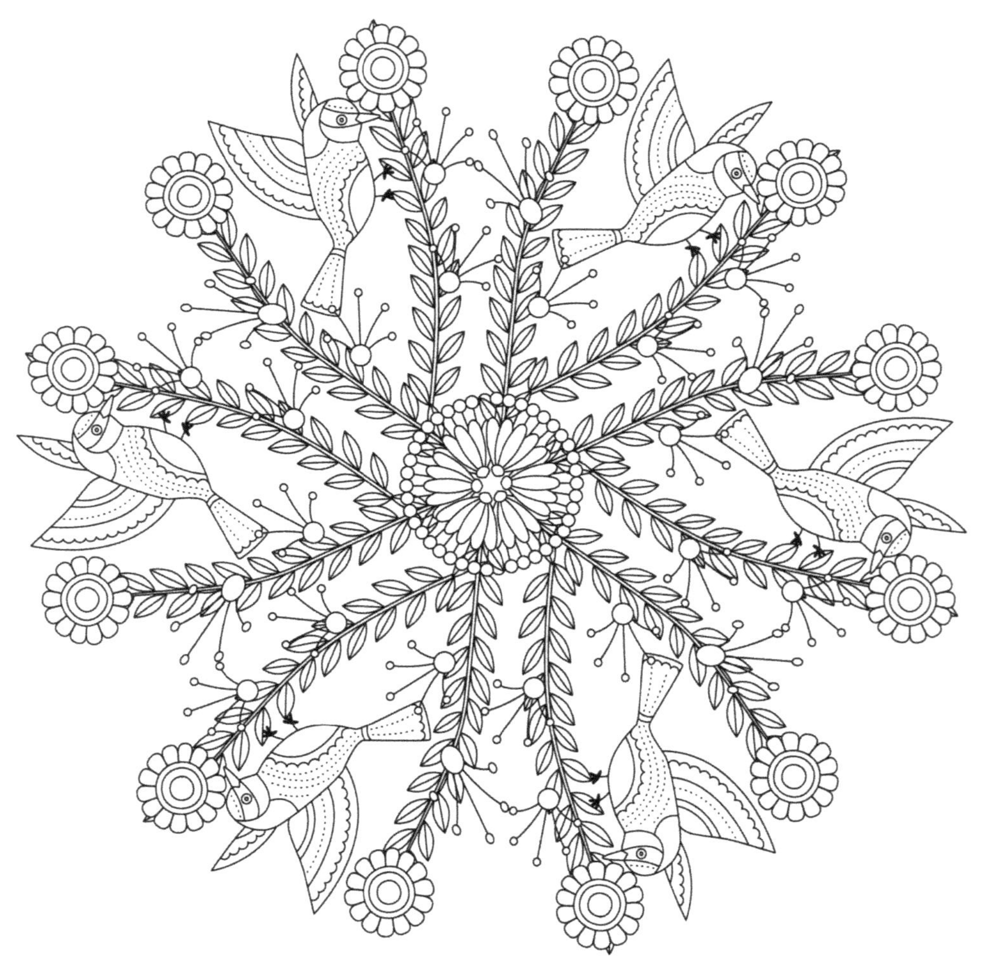

"UNLESS YOU TRY TO DO SOMETHING BEYOND
WHAT YOU'VE ALREADY MASTERED, YOU WILL NEVER GROW."
RALPH WALDO EMERSON

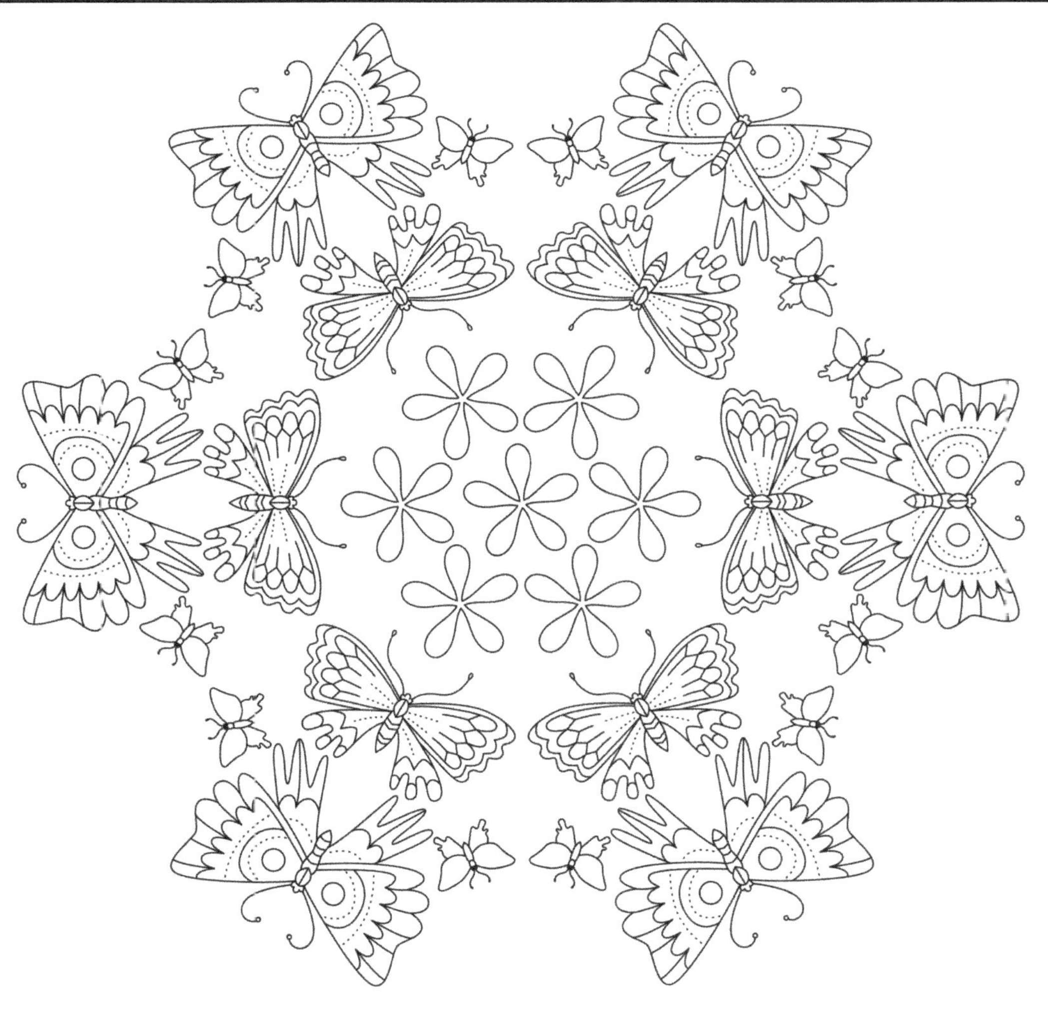

"YOU CAN'T USE UP CREATIVITY.
THE MORE YOU USE, THE MORE YOU HAVE."
MAYA ANGELOU

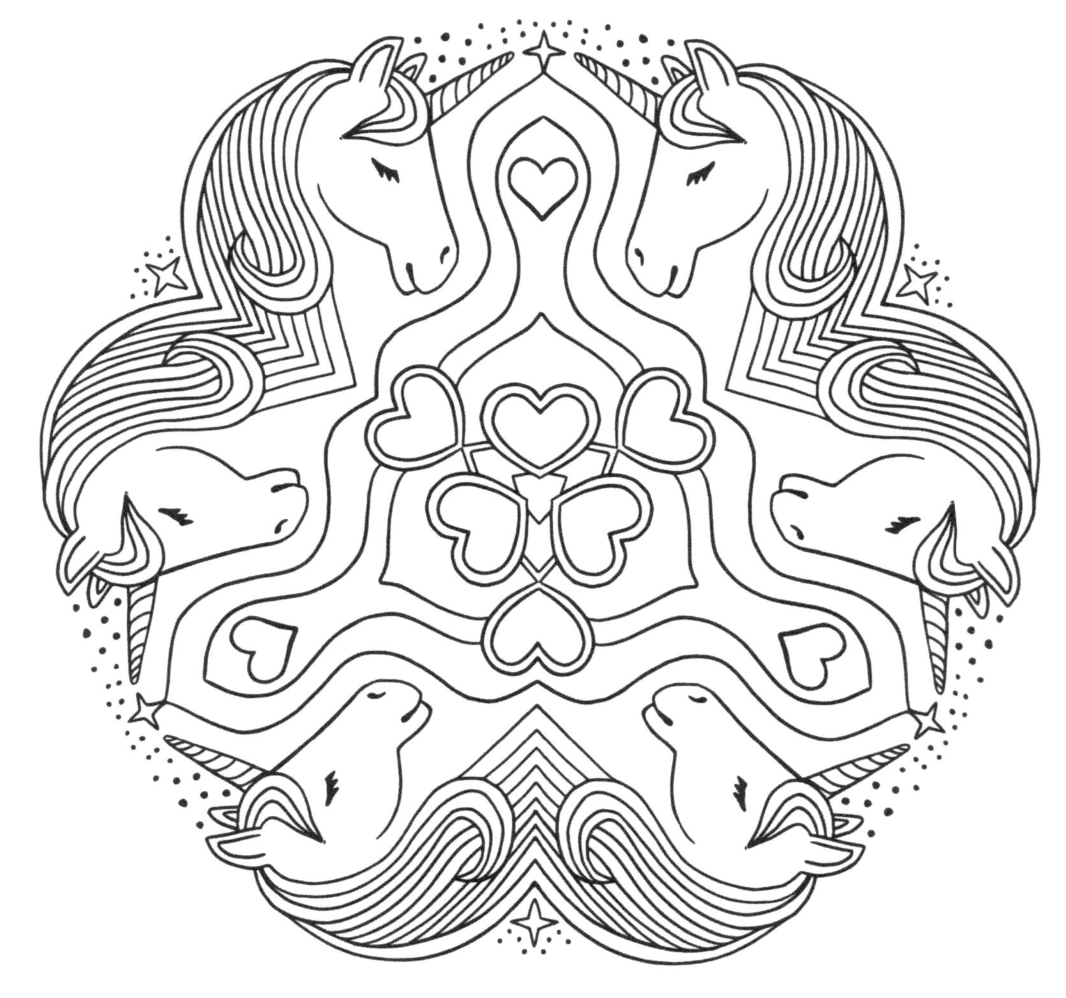

"I THINK IT'S POSSIBLE FOR ORDINARY PEOPLE
TO CHOOSE TO BE EXTRAORDINARY."
ELON MUSK

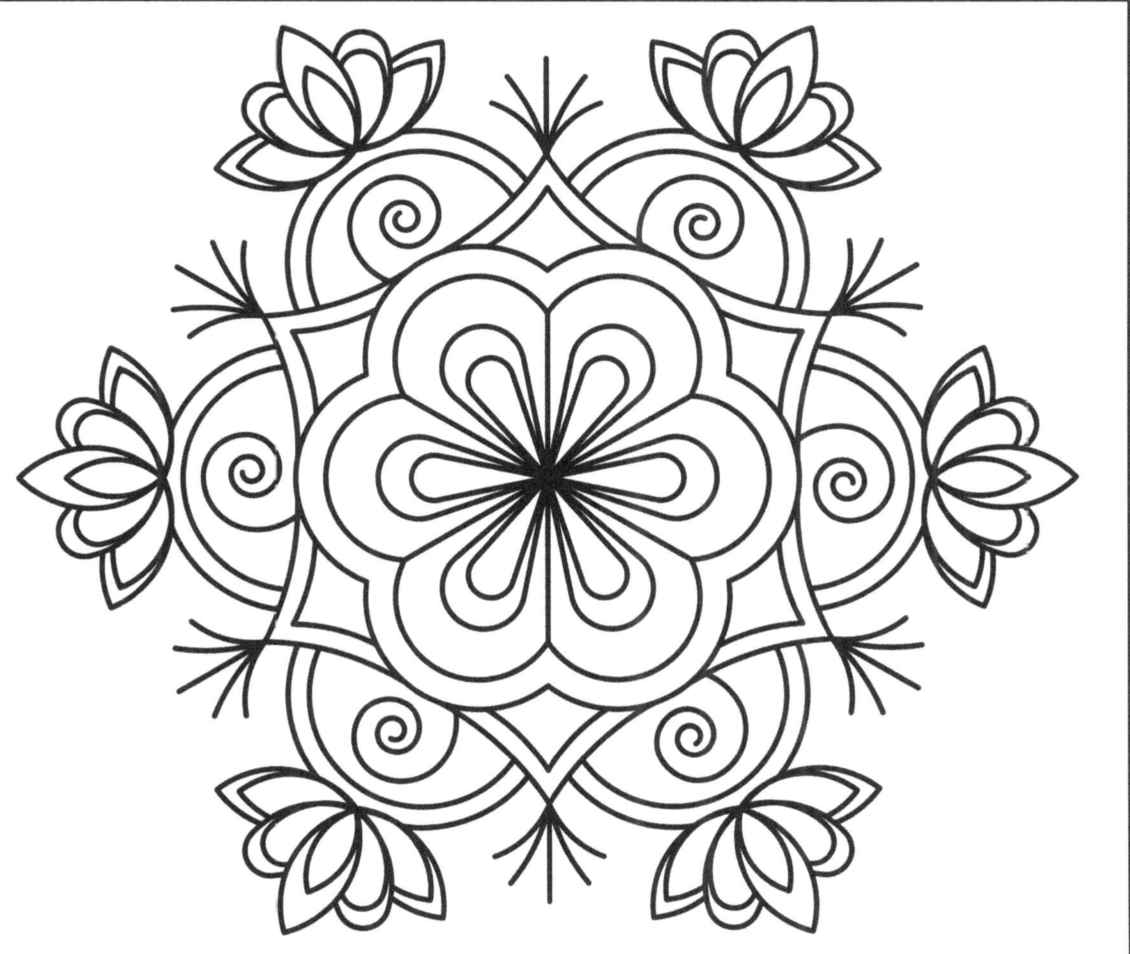

"NEVER GIVE UP ON WHAT YOU REALLY WANT TO DO.
THE PERSON WITH BIG DREAMS IS MORE POWERFUL
THAN ONE WITH ALL THE FACTS."
ALBERT EINSTEIN

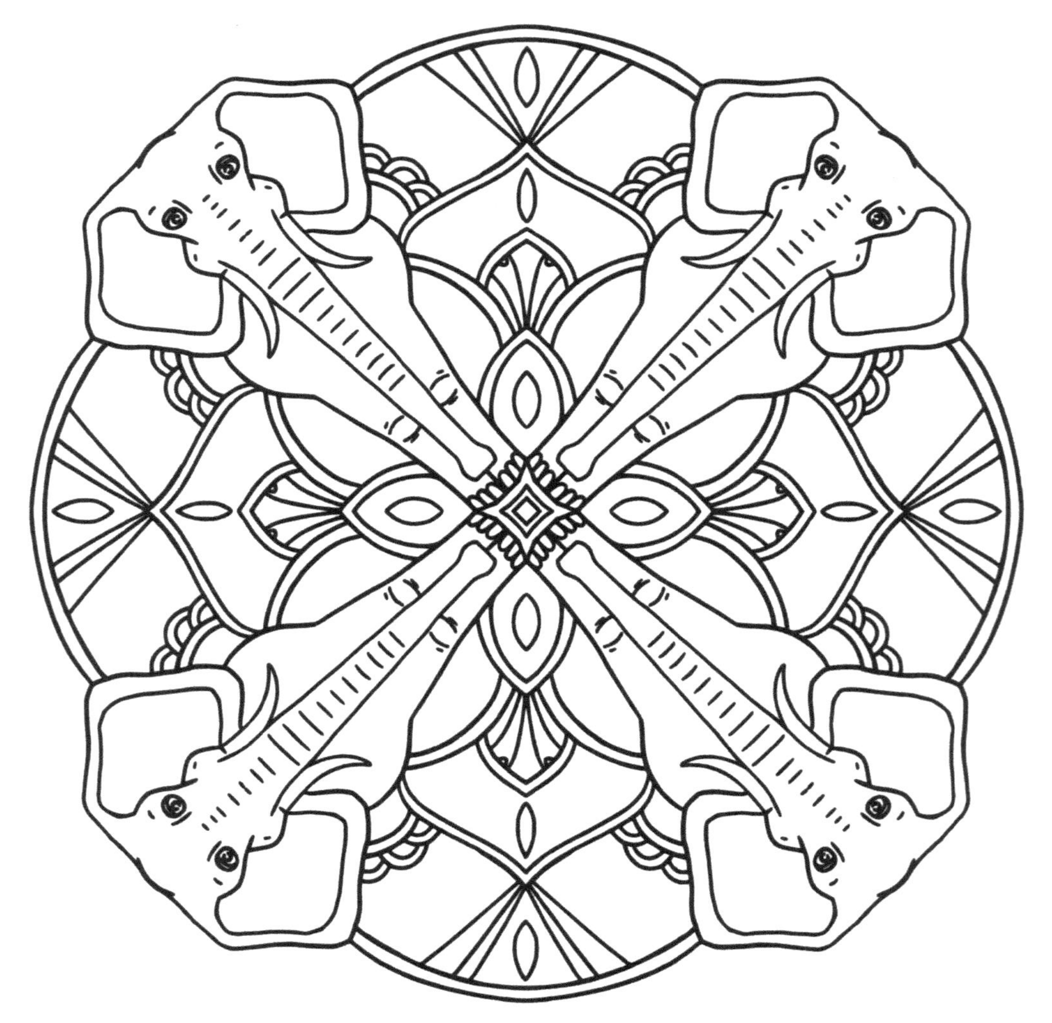

"YOU MISS 100% OF THE SHOTS YOU DON'T TAKE."
WAYNE GRETZKY

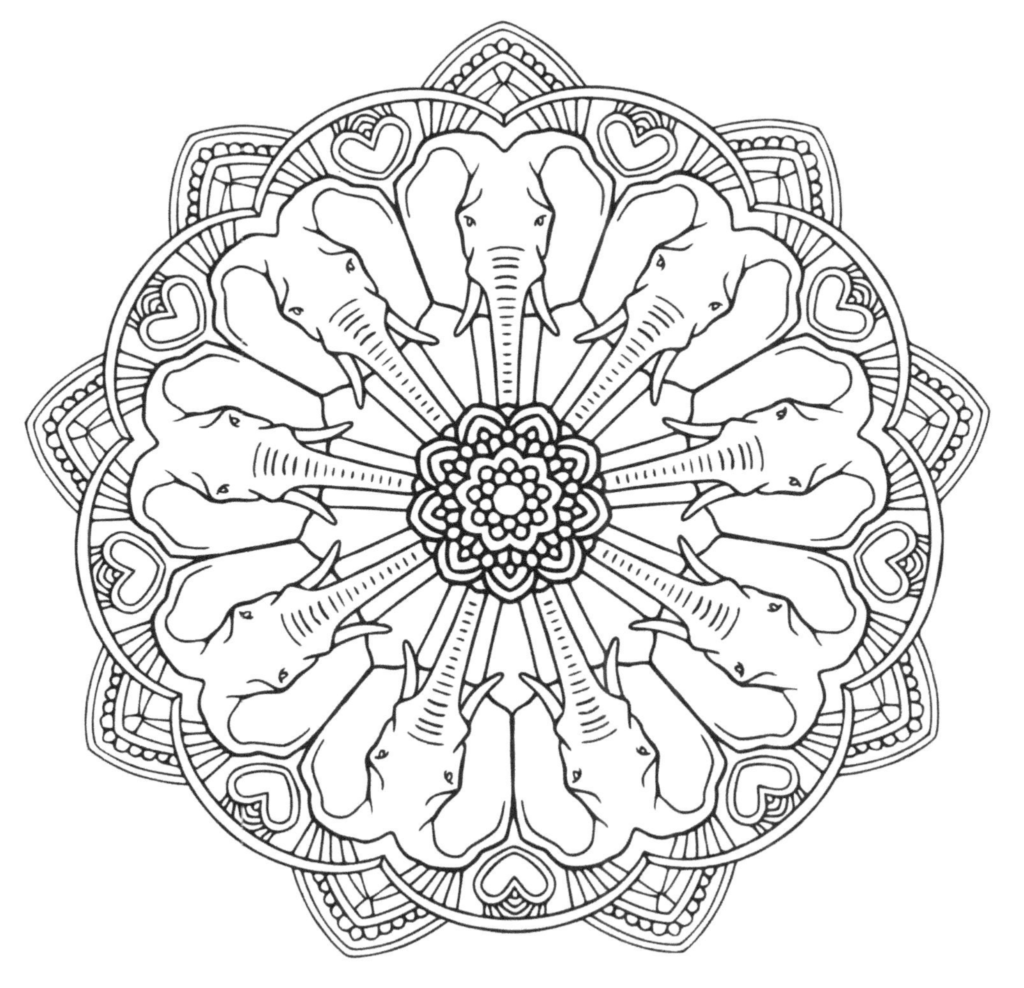

"You're braver than you believe, stronger than you seem,
and smarter than you think."
A A Milne

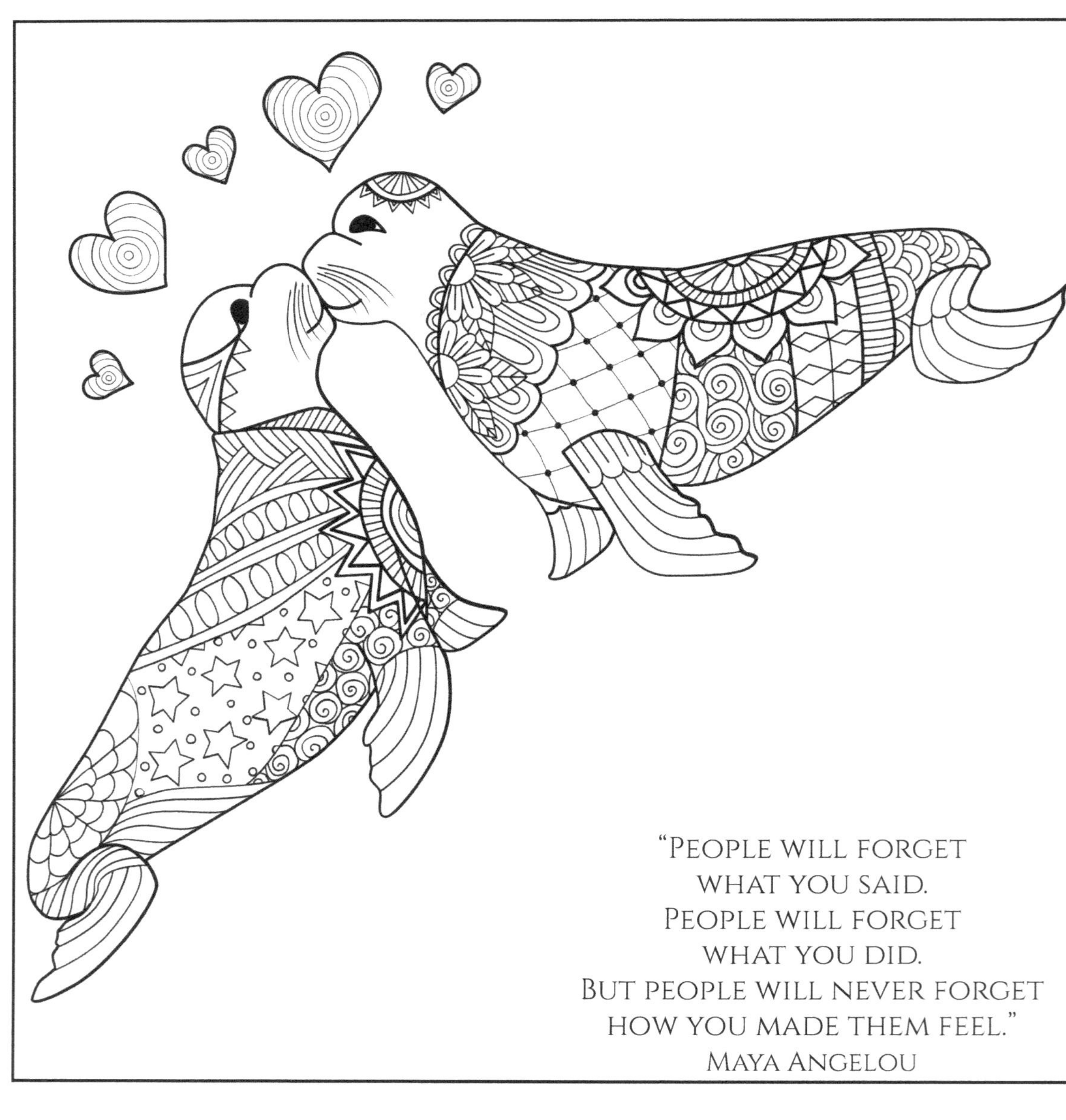
"PEOPLE WILL FORGET
WHAT YOU SAID.
PEOPLE WILL FORGET
WHAT YOU DID.
BUT PEOPLE WILL NEVER FORGET
HOW YOU MADE THEM FEEL."
MAYA ANGELOU

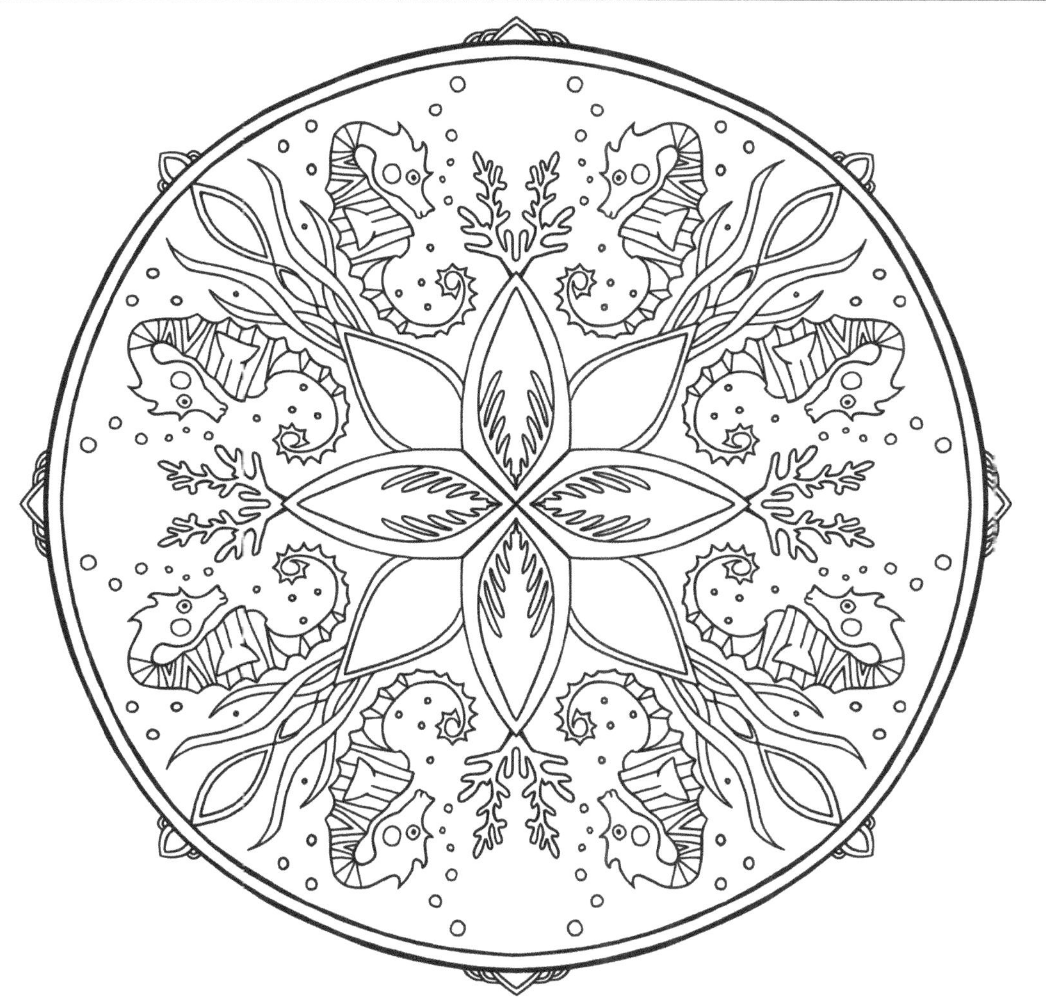

"EDUCATION IS THE KEY TO UNLOCKING THE WORLD,
A PASSPORT TO FREEDOM."
OPRAH WINFREY

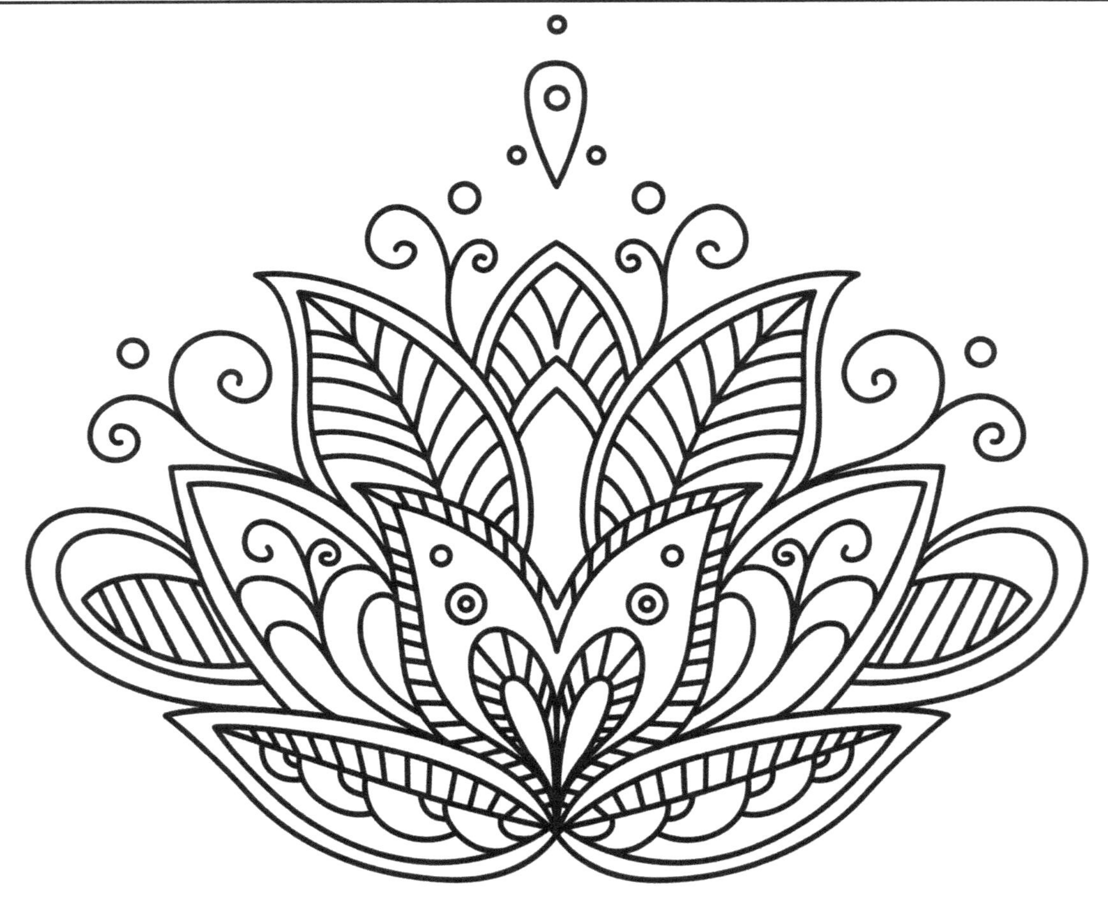

"Change will not come if we wait
for some other person or some other time.
We are the ones we've been waiting for.
We are the change that we seek."
Barack Obama

Our Story

My sister Beate and I grew up together
in West Berlin, Germany.

Our life paths led us in opposite directions;
she married and moved to India, I married and moved to the U.S.

Even though we live far apart, we are very close
and usually meet once a year in Berlin.

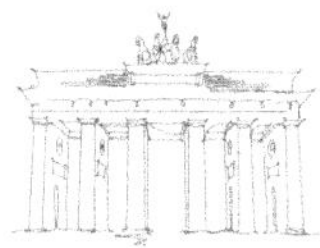

One of Beate's greatest joys is coloring mandalas,
and we started creating cards and books
in sister-Zoom sessions. This labor of love brings us
even closer together.

We hope you enjoy this book!

Love from our 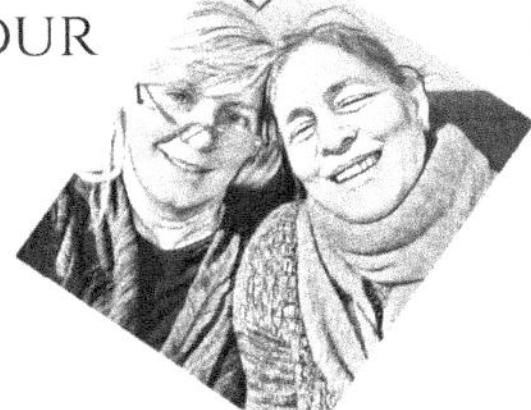 homes to yours!

Bibi   *Beate*

This book was created with Bibi LeBlanc,
best-selling author and winner of the
FAPA President's Book Award &
finalist in the *Eric Hoffer International Book Award*
for her book
Explore the Sights of Berlin Divided - Berlin United

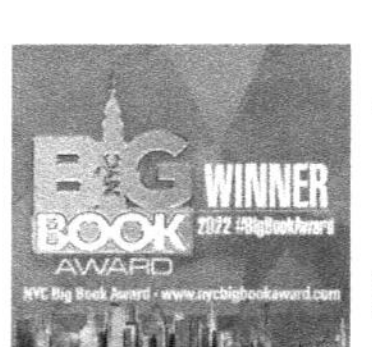
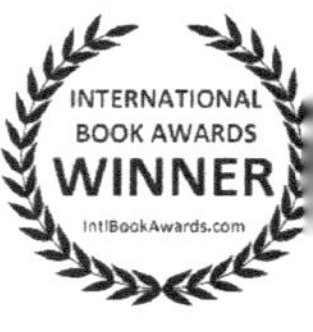

*

Kops-Fetherling International Book Award for
Discover Food & Wine of Tuscany, Italy

*

Purple Dragonfly International Book Award &
International Book Award &
IBPA Benjamin Franklin Book Award &
FAPA President's Book Award for
Endangered Animals of North America/
Bedrohte Tiere Nordamerikas

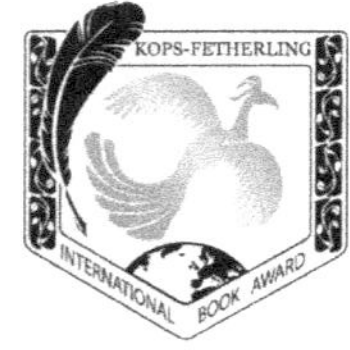
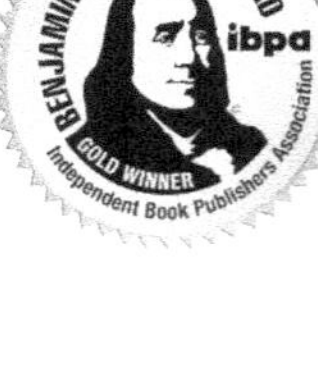

*

Next Generation International Indie Book Award &
Purple Dragonfly International Book Award &
FAPA President's Book Award for
Explore the Sights of San Francisco, Chinatown

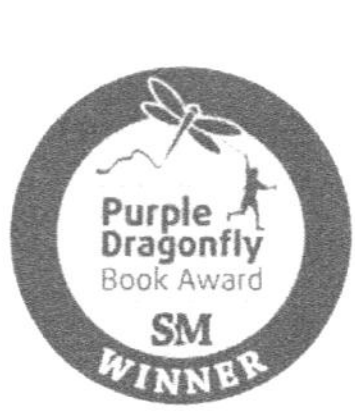
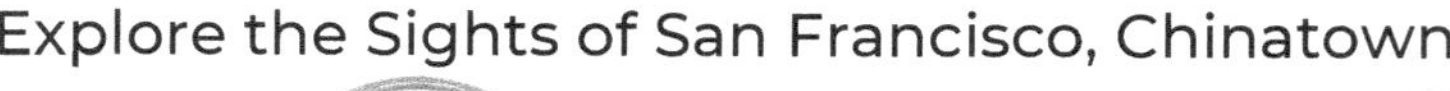
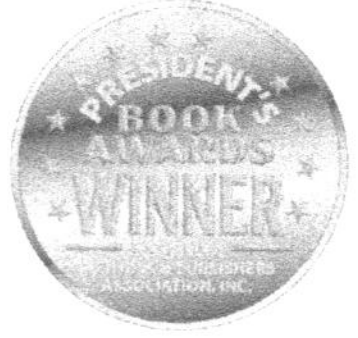
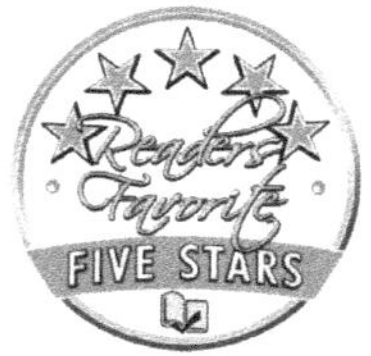
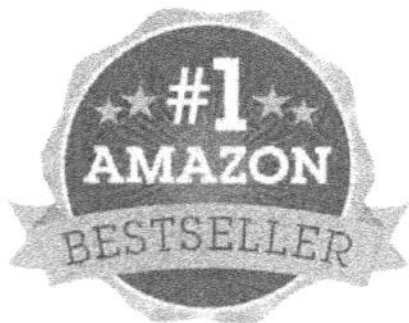
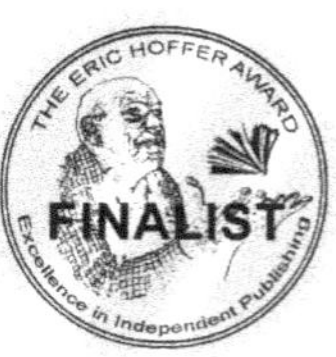

LOOKING FOR COLORING INSPIRATION OR MANDALA CARDS?

Please visit

ETSY.COM/SHOP/CULTURETOCOLOR

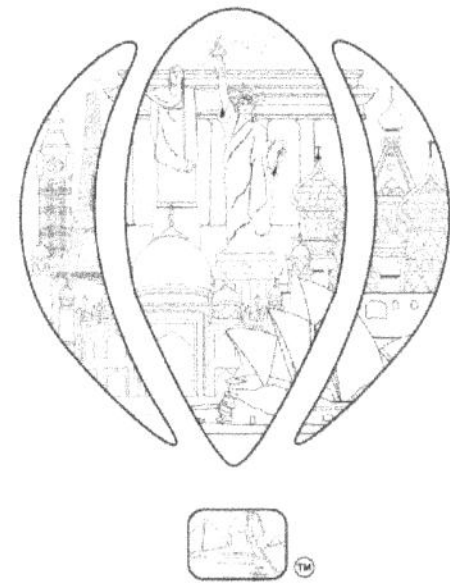

Culture to Color.com

#ConnectingCulturesThroughColoring!

About Culture to Color®

For more information visit:

CultureToColor.com

Follow us on:

f FACEBOOK.COM/CULTURETOCOLOR

◎ INSTAGRAM.COM/CULTURE_TO_COLOR

in LINKEDIN.COM/IN/BIBILEBLANC

Contact us
Bibi LeBlanc
Culture to Color, LLC®
CS@CULTURETOCOLOR.COM
+1-386-309-2632

Titles available in the Culture to Color® Mandala Series

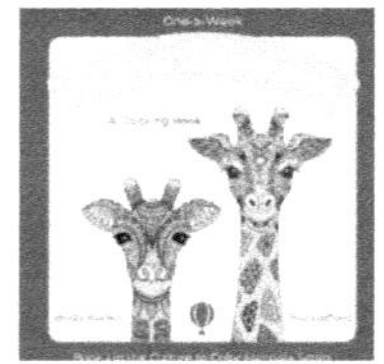 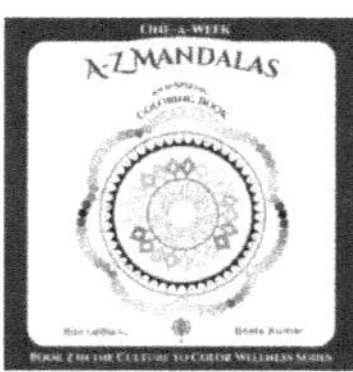 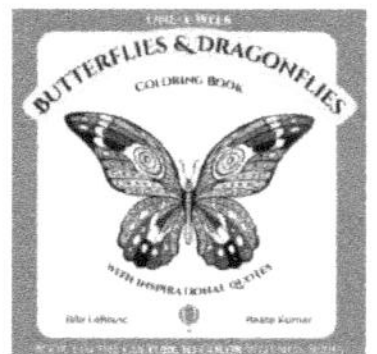 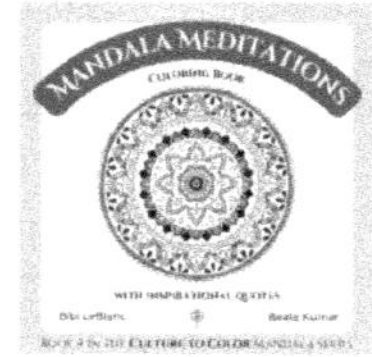 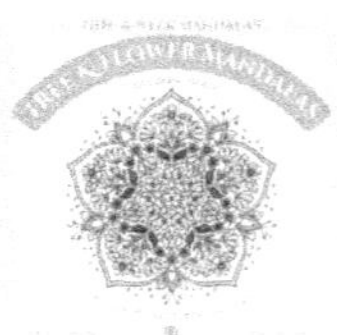

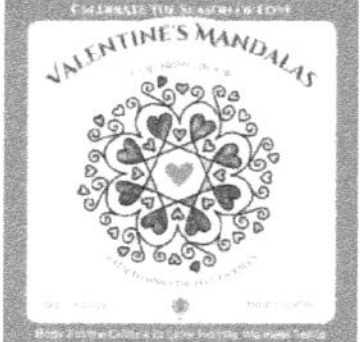 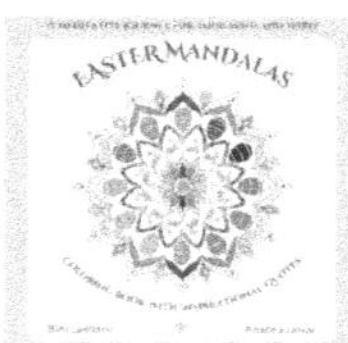 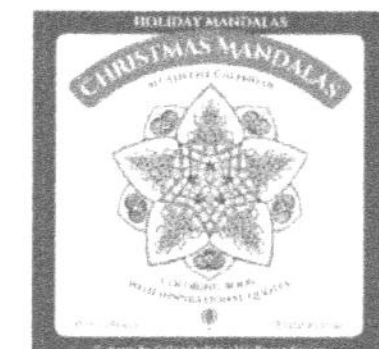

TAG US WITH YOUR COLORED PAGES #CULTURETOCOLOR